Theatre Babel presents

Educating Agnes

*a new adaptation of Molière's School for Wives,
or L'Ecole des Femmes*

by Liz Lochhead

Cast

ARNOLPHE	KEVIN McMONAGLE
AGNES	ANNEIKA ROSE
HORACE	JOHN KIELTY
CHRYSALDE	SEAN SCANLAN
ALAIN/ORANTE	LEWIS HOWDEN
GEORGETTE	MAUREEN CARR

Director and Designer	Graham McLaren
Co-Designer	Robin Peoples
Lighting Designer	Kai Fischer
Stage Manager	Yvonne Buskie
Assistant Stage Manager	Kate Frost
Administrator	Isobel Gilmour
Associate Producer	Kate Bowen
Company Manager	Rebecca Rodgers

Educating Agnes was first performed by Theatre Babel at
Citizens' Theatre, Glasgow, on 25 April 2008

COMPANY BIOGRAPHIES

Kevin McMonagle (*Arnolphe*)
Kevin trained at Drama Centre, London. He first worked with Liz Lochhead on the great Merryhell productions of *True Confessions*, *Ticklymince* and *The Pie of Damocles*; and also her magnificent tale of World War Two evacuees, *Shanghaied*.

Anneika Rose (*Agnes*)
Anneika is in her final year at RSAMD and is delighted to be working with Theatre Babel in her professional debut. Previous credits include Dandini in *Cinderella*; Rain in *Hidden*; Sonya in *Crime and Punishment*; Isabella in *Women Beware Women*; and Sofi in *Stories for a Wild Night*.

Sean Scanton (*Chrysalde*)
Sean trained at ILAN Drama Centre, London, in the 1970s. His many theatre credits include seasons at the Royal Lyceum, Edinburgh, the Bristol Old Vic, and the Sheffield Crucible. He has also worked at the Tron Theatre; the Traverse, Edinburgh; the Royal Court; the Old Vic; The Bush, London; the Mermaid, London; the Donmar Warehouse; and with the RSC at the Barbican. This will be Sean's first appearance with Theatre Babel.

John Kielty (*Horace*)
John lives between Edinburgh and San Francisco. He recently won the Highland Quest for a New Musical with *Sundowe*, which he co-wrote and performed with his band The Martians. Theatre credits include *Elizabeth Gordon Quinn* (National Theatre of Scotland); *Miseryguts*, *Victory*, *The Hypochondriak*, *Merlin* (Royal Lyceum, Edinburgh); *Observe the Sons of Ulster* (Citizens', Glasgow); *Beauty Queen of Leenanne*, *Possible Worlds* (Tron); *Caledonia Dreaming* (7:84).

Maureen Carr (*Georgette*)
Maureen's theatre credits include work at the Citizens', Glasgow; the Traverse, Edinburgh; the Tron, Glasgow; Perth Rep; Royal Lyceum, Edinburgh; and with 7:84 and Communicado theatre companies. Television and film credits include *Still Game*, *Taggart*, *Dear Green Place*, *Sea of Souls*, *Tinsel Town*, *Orphans*, *Afterlife*, and *One Life Stand* for which she won a Scottish BAFTA and Silcon New York Film Festival Award for Best Actress. This will be Maureen's first appearance with Theatre Babel.

Lewis Howden (*Alain/Orante*)

Lewis trained at RSAMD. He has worked extensively in many theatres throughout the UK and abroad. He has appeared in various films and TV dramas and has been heard in numerous radio plays. For Theatre Babel he has been seen, most recently, as the title role in *Macbeth*, and previously in *Medea* and *King Lear*.

Yvonne Buskie (Stage Manager)

Yvonne graduated from Queen Margaret College in 1994. She has worked at Edinburgh's Royal Lyceum and with many touring companies such as Plutot la Vie, Benchtours, Tosg, Communicado, Stellar Quines and Boilerhouse. As a production manager she has worked for Edinburgh Science Festival, George Square Theatre and Dancebase.

Kate Frost (Assistant Stage Manager)

Kate recently graduated from the RSAMD, where she specialised in stage management. To date, she has had a varied and successful career, including work for British Youth Opera, Scottish Youth Theatre, Scottish Youth Dance, Scottish Opera, Raymond Gubbay, and Dundee Rep Theatre.

Graham McLaren (Director and Designer)

Graham is a Glasgow-based theatre artist who has been working in professional theatre for almost two decades. In that time, he has created work ranging from totally improvised and devised work to classical texts. He has performed, designed, written, devised, taught, improvised, choreographed, programmed, directed and produced. At the age of twenty-five he established the internationally acclaimed Theatre Babel. In 2000 he started directing and designing full-time for the company, and since then his work on European classics has been seen in ancient Greek amphitheatres; black-box studios; main stages of national theatres and prestigious festivals across the world. In 2005 he was invited to join Perth Theatre, Scotland, as Creative Director. The following year he became Associate Artist for that company. In 2008 Graham joined Toronto-based theatre company Necessary Angel as Associate Artist.

Kai Fischer (Lighting Designer)
Kai has lit theatre productions for many Scottish companies including the Citizens' Theatre, Glasgow; Dundee Rep; National Theatre of Scotland; Perth Theatre; Royal Lyceum, Edinburgh; Theatre Babel; Traverse, Edinburgh; Tron, Glasgow; and Visible Fictions. Recent set and lighting design credits include *Subway, Lost Ones* (Vanishing Point); *Home (Caithness)* (National Theatre of Scotland); *Fewer Emergencies* (Ankur).

Robin Peoples (Co-Designer)
Robin was educated at the University of St Andrews. He has taught at University of Erlangen-Nurnberg, Germany. Holder of first SAC Director's Bursary; former Artistic Director of Scottish Youth Theatre and of Brunton Theatre. Robin has directed and designed over 200 productions, devised workshop and teaching materials, served on national and international committees, and commissioned over thirty plays and musical scores.

Isobel Gilmour (Administrator)
Isobel has worked in a variety of roles within arts organisations. She joined Theatre Babel in 2004 as Finance Officer and now looks after the administration of the company as well as finance and marketing.

Kate Bowen (Associate Producer)
Kate is a freelance theatre producer working with UK companies and directors. Prior to working independently, she was Babel's Executive Producer, producing seven international and twelve domestic tours, and overseeing the development of the company from 1999 to 2007.

Rebecca Rodgers (Company Manager)
Rebecca trained at RSAMD. Co-founder of Theatre Babel, she has been company manager for almost all of Babel's tours and appeared in nearly all of Babel's productions, appearing as Juliet in *Romeo and Juliet*; Ophelia in *Hamlet*; Olivia in *Twelfth Night*; Regan in *King Lear*; Chorus in *Medea*; Hippolita in *'Tis Pity She's a Whore*; Nora in *A Doll's House* and Lady Macbeth in *Macbeth*.

Theatre Babel

Theatre Babel work with collaborators from different disciplines to liberate some of the world's greatest plays, igniting the imagination of artists to explore the truth and release the extraordinary in classic myths and dramas. They create opportunities for artists to cross mediums and ignore traditional boundaries applied to classical drama.

Theatre Babel constantly redefines their approach to creating work and seeks new ways to surprise themselves and their audiences. The evolution of the company's practice has led to site-specific epic commissions from multiple playwrights, engaging songwriters, puppeteers and poets, developing chorus work over months of rehearsals, working in ancient Greek amphitheatres, black-box studios and the main stages of national theatres across the world.

Their recent work has included shows based on the plays of Ibsen, Shakespeare, Euripides and Ben Jonson. Graham McLaren, who co-founded the company when he was twenty-five, designs and directs most of the productions, working with a UK-wide collective of performers, designers, writers and musicians. They create work on a number of scales – from one-man plays to productions that have performed on number-one stages; as well as site-specific and outdoor performances.

Theatre Babel is based in Glasgow and they exploit the rich resources of the city's many performance spaces to develop their work. Their work is intrinsically reflective of and responsive to Scottish culture.

Theatre Babel tour extensively and their shows travel throughout the UK to a range of venues. Their work overseas has spanned three continents.

Theatre Babel
PO Box 5103
Glasgow
G78 9AR
Scotland UK

tel: **+44 (0)141 634 3030**
e-mail: **admin@theatrebabel.co.uk**
web: **www.theatrebabel.co.uk**

Theatre Babel are a registered charity SCO 022739
Company Registration No 151573 | VAT Registration No 6716108 41

Director's Note

I remember very clearly the day Liz Lochhead and I started the journey that has led to the script you now have in your hand.

I was giving her a lift home to her flat in the west end of Glasgow after some show or dinner or, God forbid, some industry event that I have since erased from my memory. I was telling Liz that I was planning to create a version of *The Country Wife* by Wycherley. I had barely finished the sentence when she said, 'Don't!' I said, 'What? Don't you like it?' She said, 'No, not really, but that's not the point – I'll do a new adaptation of a European classic for you instead...'

And that statement (for it wasn't really a request) hung in the air for enough time for me to remember:

- How much I regretted declining her very kind offer to work on *Hedda Gabler* a few years previously. (The thought even now makes me cringe.)
- The extraordinary time we have had, across the world, working on European classics in the past.
- How blessed I was to have such a remarkable and talented artist wanting to create a show with me.

All of the above took seconds, but clearly still too long for Liz. She added, 'It'll be my present to you.'

Of course I said yes.

It wasn't long before we had settled on a Molière, and on *L'Ecole des Femmes*.

It has indeed been a wonderful present to me. The script, as it made its way to me in almost weekly installments, has made me laugh and really cheered me up in the last year; I realise only now that that is something Liz thought I needed. I only hope I can do it justice in production.

For those of you reading the script without having seen it produced, I really hope it makes you laugh as much as it has me.

Graham McLaren
Artistic Director
Theatre Babel

March 2008

EDUCATING AGNES

translated and adapted by
Liz Lochhead

from Molière's *L'Ecole des Femmes*

Introduction

Today was the first day of rehearsals. Into production and its
own theatrical life, whatever it may prove to be, goes *Educating
Agnes*; this particular new version, mine for Theatre Babel, of
the first of Molière's great verse comedies, *L'Ecole des
Femmes*. The play about an old man of forty-two who is so
obsessed with the infidelity and treachery of womankind he
decides the solution is to marry a young, young girl – his ward,
a child innocent to the point of ignorance – and, all the worse
for him, falls in love with her. The play which Molière, leading
actor, wrote for himself when he was forty, newly married to the
beautiful seventeen-year-old actress Armande Béjart, 'little
sister' (no, daughter, many said) of his long-time lover and
fellow company-member Madéleine. (Incest, many said, specu-
lating scandalously on the paternity of 'the daughter'...) Newly
married and only just at the beginning of the agonies of the
sexual jealousy he'd suffer for the rest of his life with the apparently pathologically faithless Armande. Indeed, she was supposed to be the model for the lovely and wicked Célimène, who
causes such agonies to the protagonist in his later masterpiece
Le Misanthrope...

Today it turns out to be a particularly exuberant read-through,
and there is an amazingly strong – and for a first day, an
almost uncannily tight-knit – company feeling among the six
actors. Though all are Scottish, they haven't ever worked
together, or even met each other, before. Kevin McMonagle is
almost as terrifying as he is hilarious in his intensity; and, as
long as we can refrain from telling him which bits we find particularly disgusting, disturbing or funny (this always ruins
such moments), looks set to be a brilliant Arnolphe. I can't
wait to see how far he will take it. Anneika Rose – tiny, beautiful, black, Glaswegian and an absolutely outstanding student,
still in her final year at the Royal Scottish Academy of Music

and Dramatic Art – has been released to play Agnes in our production. As I began my version a year ago, I was thinking it might just be interesting to have a black or Asian actress to point up further a colonial – as well as the inherent patriarchal and paternalistic – sexual exploitation (one which would, of course, never be mentioned) of the orphaned ward. It was then I saw Anneika win, at the RSAMD, the Duncan Macrae Medal for the Speaking of Scots; coincidentally – no, fatefully, I thought – with a speech of Agnes's from *Let Wives Tak Tent* (The classic Scots prose translation of *L'Ecole des Femmes*). Graham McLaren, the producer and director of Babel, wasn't particularly enamoured of my 'black Agnes' idea, but when he saw Anneika, her talent and extraordinary truthfulness won him over.

I feel blessed and lucky to be back in a rehearsal room with Graham, who has given me another chance to be as cheeky and radical as I want with a great classic. Indeed, only last week he was pushing me to be a bit less reverent with Molière's ending; one which he's convinced Molière would have done slightly better had he written this play after *Le Tartuffe* or *Le Misanthrope*. 'If you stick with the suffering of Arnolphe to the last moment of the play, it'll be a lot more satisfying for the audience,' he urged.

'Stick with the suffering' is of course essentially good advice for anyone working on any comedy worth its salt.

It's strange, though, to be here with a version of one Molière play I thought I'd never do. You can't work on one of these comedies in this country without realising you are part of a long and popular tradition of Molière in Scotland. Sixty years ago, the legendary Duncan Macrae took to the stage in Edinburgh in a role which had been written especially for him: that of Oliphant (Molière's Arnolphe) in that previously mentioned ground-breaking, and tradition-forging, 'free translation' of *L'Ecole des Femmes* in Lallans ('braid Scots', some will have it) by Robert Kemp, *Let Wives Tak Tent* (an archaism which means something like 'Hey, women, be careful, pay attention, watch out, beware!').

This, the first of many 'MacMolières' from several different
Scots playwrights over the years, has remained a well-loved
classic, being produced as recently as 2001 at Pitlochry Festival
Theatre. It is, as are most of the incarnations of *L'Ecole des
Femmes* – it is just such a very funny play – a perennial
favourite with audiences. In the early 1980s it was revived by
the short-lived Scottish Theatre Company with the inimitable
Rikki Fulton inheriting the central role.

That was the first Molière I ever saw, as part of a laughing-long-
and-loud capacity audience in Glasgow's Kings Theatre. In
terms of language, the title was probably the most difficult thing
about it, and, live and listening, the audience had no problem
with the intelligibility of what, on the page, can look to be a
rather antique if richly textured Scots.

Though I only actually read this play in its entirety last week, I
had always felt that it had claimed the territory.

Of course, I have read other versions; my favourite being the
lovely Derek Mahon one, with its elegant, inventive rhymes
and ease of utterance. He very kindly gave me a copy – I
might have swapped it for a copy of my then-recent *Tartuffe*?
– almost twenty years ago after we met by chance in the
Chelsea Arts Club and had a conversation about our mutual
love of Molière. Another reason for me not to attempt a
School for Wives.

What changed my mind? Well, Graham McLaren and I had
been looking to make a new version of a great classic comedy
from world theatre, performable by six or less actors for Babel,
now. (We really wanted, needed, a comedy after all these Greek
tragedies we'd worked on together over the past few years.) We
looked at all the other Molières in the form I always work from,
the original (flowery 'f's for 's's, et al) on one side of the
double-page spread, with contemporary seventeenth-, or occa-
sionally eighteenth-century literals in English on the other. The
freshness and pertinence of *L'Ecole des Femmes* was irresistible. Particularly as I thought it would actually be possible to
turn Henrique into an *offstage*-character and then, not to the
scene's detriment either, Chrysalde and Orante alone could

easily together effect the almost *deus-ex-machina* function of the ending. We could well cut out the 'notary' figure (was there someone in Molière's company who specialised in lawyer turns and wanted to be in everything?); I thought a mere tweak could make the maid Georgette insolently *mock*-stupid and more of a prototype for Molière's later Dorine and Toinette; I could see a nifty way of making a more attractive and equal part for a good actor, by double-casting daft man-servant Alain, and Orante. So, six players...

Kemp says, 'The problems of translation from French are in some ways heightened when it becomes a question of transmuting the rhymed Alexandrines of an evenly accented tongue to a heavily stressed dialect of the Teutonic group.' and although I'm with him on this, I still fundamentally disagree with his decision that it is 'best to aim at an idiomatic Scottish prose.'

Au contraire, when Molière rhymes, I think the translation really ought to as well.

Are we recreating the effect of Alexandrines in French? Not at all. But there is something about the energy that rhyming – whether in Scots, English or American – gives to the text and the actors. There is something fundamentally *comic* about rhyme, particularly with polysyllabic feminine rhymes or outrageous near-rhymes – I, personally, would hesitate to attempt a rhyming *Phèdre*, although the late great Scottish dramatist and translator Robert David MacDonald actually did a beautiful, speakable one in Standard English couplets.

At any rate I decided that, as *Let Wives* was sixty years old, and I was about to be too, I could, as a sixtieth birthday present to myself, allow myself the treat of making the version I had so long resisted.

Molière is arguably the world's greatest comic playwright. His plays are 'universal in their application yet untranslatable', according to a snooty contributor to *The Oxford Companion to the Theatre*, who believes that, 'In transit the wit evaporates and only a skeleton plot is left. This, however,' he writes ruefully, 'will not deter people from trying.'

No, it won't. For the Liverpool Everyman and Playhouse, and their Year of Culture, my friend Roger McGough has just made his own brand-new rhyming-version of *Tartuffe*, and that'll be happening at the same time as my new *L'Ecole des Femmes*.

But as I've already said, we Scots playwrights in particular, from Kemp onwards, have been much guiltier than others of this supposedly foolhardy exercise, and it is fun to speculate on the reasons for this perennially resprouting branch of the Auld Alliance. Is it because we have no plays of our own from this time? Are we filling a gap? Certainly, our Reformation, early and thorough, stamped out all drama and dramatic writing for centuries. This means that the indigenous product seems to consist of Lyndsay's 1540 *Ane Satyre of the Thrie Estaites* – and 'ane satire' is definitely not enough. We have no Scottish Jacobean tragedies, no Scottish Restoration Comedies. Our greatest dramatist that never was, Burns, confined himself to the dramatic monologue purely in poetic form. The characters he created were only given rein in the multiple lyric voices of his many conflicting personae. Holy Willie and Tartuffe may be brother archetypes, but only one had a full five-act play written about him.

But why Molière? What is there about this particular seventeenth-century Frenchman that has made him our darling? Well, for one thing, he's a lot funnier than Corneille or Racine, and our great Scottish theatre actors have tended to be comedians.

Critics talk about the vigour of his language, his mixture of current cliché, colloquialism, earthy talk with the high-flown. All varieties and shades of Scots, from the classical eighteenth-century language of Burns and Ferguson, to the despised (oh, not by me!) modern urban varieties have this – often vulgar, but very real and undeniable – vernacular vigour. Scottish people are very used to shifting registers, and even varieties of the Scottish accent and usage, without very much in the way of special Scots vocabulary is arguably still a lot more robust than 'standard English' as a medium for the translation of comic rhyme. The different characters in my versions of Molière might all be Scottish in their speech, but speak differently from one other: maids don't speak like masters, although masters might often, for their own purposes, choose to speak like maids. My three different Molière versions over the years have been in very different theatrical languages from each other, in various shades and degrees of Scots.

More than twenty years ago as I worked on *Tartuffe,* it came out (and no one was more surprised than I was) in the robustly Lowland Scots tongue of my Lanarkshire granny. No one, Scots or English – or even French – in the audience ever complained at all of intelligibility, and it has been frequently revived; last time in a twentieth-anniversary production at its original home, the Royal Lyceum in Edinburgh. By contrast, when I did *Le Misanthrope*, as *Miseryguts*, for the same theatre in 2002, that play seemed to demand to be set in a specific, here-and-now Edinburgh media-world, and its language was even more rife with Americanisms, clichés, buzzwords and casual profanity than with Scotticisms – of which, nevertheless, there are many.

Educating Agnes? It feels to me to be different again. I'm just as confident it'll make sense in the Oxford Playhouse as it will in the Glasgow Citizens. But it's a very Scottish version for this very Scottish cast of actors and for this company – Theatre Babel – which has had this long commitment to making classical work that is strongly rooted here and to taking it out to the wider world.

Of course my hopes and dreams for this version are that it will eventually be done by other companies, both professional and amateur, in England and other parts of the English-speaking world too. Then Arnolphe will (for instance) say: 'Thanks for the eloquent harangue / You're right. I'm obviously *wrong*.' It'll be a half-rhyme instead of a full one. Instead of 'ain two sels' – already a deliberately 'half-and-hauf' construction to characterise his pawkily ingratiating use of Scots – Chrysalde will say 'own two selves'. And it'll be none the worse for that. There might be seven actors instead of six if the company can afford not to double – though they'll lose the fun our Lewis Howden is having contrasting the thickest, lowest-class servant Alain with the grandest, high-status, orotund Orante, who arrives to sort everything out.

Molière's comedy is profound, universal and eternal. What he reveals here about the power-relationships between old men and young girls – about unhealthy obsession, about youth, sweetness and innocence versus middle-aged male self-deception, terror of sex and misogyny – are, of course, all equally pertinent today. Beyond all that though, it is – as are both of those other masterpieces of his I have come to know and love so well – finally about the comical, appalling suffering which love, especially inappropriate love, causes us human beings.

Liz Lochhead
25 March 2008

Miseryguts *and* Tartuffe *are published in one volume by NHB*

Characters

CHRYSALDE
ARNOLPHE
ALAIN
GEORGETTE
AGNES
HORACE
ORANTE

This text went to press before the end of rehearsals and so may differ slightly from the play as performed.

ACT ONE

*Early morning. Two middle-aged gentlemen, one apparently
cocky and superior (*ARNOLPHE*) – returning with bags from a
trip – and his friend (*CHRYSALDE*) are walking through a
provincial town, towards* ARNOLPHE*'s front door, where they
pause.*

CHRYSALDE.
  You are going to *marry* her? Don't say –

ARNOLPHE.
  Yup. I'm going to post the Banns the day!

CHRYSALDE.
  We're here by our ain two sel's, sir, overheard
  By nobody, nowhere. So permit me just a word?
  As your true pal, my friend, I worry for you.
  If you insist on going through with this I'm sorry for you.
  You are not the type for matrimony, I fear.
  Between you, me and the bedpost it's a really crap idea.

ARNOLPHE.
  Can be! Was for *you*, Chrysalde, that I don't doubt,
  But not everybody's wife's compelled, like yours, to put it
      about.

CHRYSALDE.
  Ouch! Well, it happens and it need not be the worst...
  I won't be the last just as no way I'm the first.
  I take the philosophical view because you can't prevent it.
  If you're going to be cuckolded, no way to circumvent it.
  Horns hurt, yup, when you're forced to wear 'em.
  They sting, the sins of the spouse, when you're forced to
      grin and bear 'em.
  Oh, you may laugh, but if you get married, mate,
  You might find your laughter's maybe tempting fate?

ARNOLPHE.

So the husband hereabouts pretends he's cool
About it – as if that makes him somehow No One's Fool?
Honestly, this town! Must every man be such a wimp
As to take what's dished out to him and be so bloody *limp*
About fighting back in any way? One man's rich
But his wife spends it all on her lover, the bitch!
Another hasn't a bean but, blatantly, his wife
Has plenty – the spoils of a pure and virtuous life
Of chastely withheld favours, I don't think!
A third chap won't take it lying down, kicks up a stink
But as well save his breath for all the good it does him.
Another refuses to let her infidelity phase him
And, when loverboy comes calling, doesn't let it get his goat
But '*pops out for a quick one*', picking up his hat and coat.
One wily wife makes her poor-sap-of-a-man '*her confidante*'
Over the attentions of some young guy – which she does
    not want –
Oh no, not much! – but that's her husband suckered. Nice!
The happily married man? Fool's paradise!
You have to laugh!

CHRYSALDE.

        That's true.
As long as you accept the world may someday laugh at you!
Oh, I know how it is. Yup. Folk Will Talk.
Maybe it's my own marital misfortunes make me baulk
At taking even passing pleasure in another's pains.
Cheap laughs like that? Well, no one gains
Owt by 'em. Call me po-faced but I can't be annoyed
By prurient indulgence in *schadenfreude* –
No, especially as he who indulges in it
Actually does not bloody know the minute!
So let them laugh behind my back at my disgrace
Because I'd rather that than have them laughing in my face.
– Though some are so genuinely sympathetic
They keep their pity to themselves – for I'd call him pathetic
Who has to openly and publicly confront his shame
Wouldn't you, sir? Oh, *your* wife's Good Name –

If you had one – would be a commodity just as volatile
And the loss of it would make the whole town smile.

ARNOLPHE.
Forget it. Worry not 'bout me on that score!
I've… eh… duh! worked all this out before.
I know what like women are, Chrysalde my friend,
They are the pits! They are the living end!
And men are at the mercy of their cheating ways
But *I*… well, I'm going to spend my days
– And nights – with one who doesn't know what's meant
By cheating, she's so young and innocent.

CHRYSALDE.
You kid yourself that some kid –

ARNOLPHE.
                              No, I
Don't kid myself about anything, here's why:
Wives like your one, those with all the smarts,
The ballbreakers, they're the ones to break our hearts.
So no bluestocking bride for me – there's a very fine line
Between brainy and barmy, so a burd that's no Einstein,
That's the best and only hope for a happy alliance.
Yes, pick a simple girl – it's not rocket science!
No, she needn't be good at just one thing, but it
S'enough if she can love *me* – and Jesus! – and can sew
        and knit.

CHRYSALDE.
By simple you mean…?

ARNOLPHE.
                         – Not *challenged* in any way,
Not a *divv* nor a daftie or… *lacking*, as we used to say.
God! Take some beautiful brainbox, and, I tell you, I'd
        prefer
Plain-as-a-scone and thick-as-a-plank to her!

CHRYSALDE.
But beauty! Irresistible when adorned by wit!

ARNOLPHE.

Give me plain goodness and you keep it.

CHRYSALDE.

But this simple, not to say simpleton, this *saint*,
How has she the *sense* to be good? Your argument
Falls down on that one – gotcha, brother!
Besides you'd not be good for one another –
The intellectually ill-matched are incompatible, well-known
     fact!
Besides: the clever would-be adulteress won't be caught in
     the act –
She knows full-well it's wrong! But your sweet little fool
Doesn't know what she's at, so she's easy to pull!

ARNOLPHE.

You can talk at me till you're blue in the face
But you won't budge me. Watch this space,
I'm going to marry a sweet, pure, simple girl
Because your intellectual types, they make my toes curl.

CHRYSALDE.

I'll say no more!

ARNOLPHE.

                    Don't! I don't mean to blame
You – but it wouldnae dae if we were aw the same,
Eh, would it? Hey, Chrysalde, you know I'm well-off
So I don't need to marry for money but for... love
You could say, not to get too flowery, ha-ha!
Don't start! Yes, I'm old enough to be her papa.
So what! In fact I've been *in loco parentis*
Since she was a wean and I had an apprentice
Affection for my wee lamb Agnes, even then.
Wee doll, so she was, at nine or ten!
That was all the age she was when her paternal granny
     died –
Not that I had any inkling then she'd one day be my bride –
But the wee soul in all the wide world was all alone.
Well, I couldn't bring her up all on my own

So it was a case of the nuns – I know! – and a convent school
And brought up to be loving and obedient, no fool,
But sweet and *very* grateful. Now, I think I could attract her
Even if I was not her one and only benefactor
But she knows, does my Agnes, who foots the bills,
Buys her food, her frocks, every silly folderol that fills
Her innocent wee heart with childish pleasure.
The nuns did her proud – there is no measure
Of what that girl does not know, her utter purity
Of heart – despite her physical maturity,
Because my innocent wee pet's almost *eighteen*!
Time to bring her home, not under *my roof*, I mean
Thon wouldn't be right, there's folk in and out,
Bad influences – and there would be talk, no doubt
Of imaginary, I assure you, impropriety.
No, I've set her up practically next door here, in the sole
     society
Of a couple who're respectable (if as daft as hersel)
And – till we're married – this arrangement'll do very well.
Come for your supper, meet my intended and you'll see
How excellent my choice is. No flies on me!

CHRYSALDE.

I'll be there! You've painted quite a picture
Of this…

ARNOLPHE.

       Simply perfect creature!
Oh, she's a duck, she's a lamb, you have to laugh!
I marvel at it, I mean, *innocent*? No half!
What will she come out with next? You'll never believe
What she said to me the other day – is this not naïve? –
'You know *babies*, Uncle?' 'Yes, my dear…'
'Is it true that they are born out of the lady's ear?'

CHRYSALDE.

Priceless such ignorance, Arnolphe, it's hard to credit –

ARNOLPHE.

Don't call me *Arnolphe*, it's *de la Touche*, geddit?

CHRYSALDE.

>Sorry, sorry, Arn – de la Touche! – ma mooth
>Finds it hard to get roon that one, that's the truth!
>This changing-your-name thing's all the style!
>Did you hear boot the mechanic changed his name to 'de l'Ile'?
>*Ile*! *Oil*! As in WD – fuckit, forget it, never mind!
>Just… this carry-on's a wee bitty pretentious, I find?

ARNOLPHE.

>Pretentious? *Moi?* Your objections are superfluous
>Because 'de la Touche' to my ear sounds more mellifluous.

CHRYSALDE.

>But all your life long, you've been Arnolphe!
>You're Arnolphe at the Rotary, Arnolphe at the Golf,
>At the *Kirk*, at the *Lodge* – you were Arnolphe at the school!
>But now you've got a few bob, this damn-fool
>Taking-a-title, trying-to-sound-posh, new-fangled fashion –
>Up to yourself, but! *Be* de la Touche, smashin!
>Just that we can't get used to it, we forget,
>Call you Arnie, or Arnolphe, and you get upset!

ARNOLPHE.

>I've worked hard all my life, Chrysalde, and every bean
>   I've got
>Has been hard-earned by my own hard work, the lot!
>It was hard, bloody hard – oh, but it was a scoosh
>To change my name last year by deed poll to de la Touche.

CHRYSALDE.

>We just can't get used to de la Touche, Arnolphe!
>Even your letters still come addressed to your old self.

ARNOLPHE.

>I can take it from those who Just Don't Know
>But you –

CHRYSALDE.

>   Very remiss of me, that's so!
>I'm sorry! My dear Arnolphe, all my days
>I'll make sure it's de la Touche, always.

And CHRYSALDE *makes a gesture of farewell, starts to go.* ARNOLPHE, *instead of entering his own imposing front door, makes for that of the little house across the square which, he has indicated, is the place* AGNES *is domiciled.*

ARNOLPHE.
Cheeribye then, I'll… eh… just knock
And make sure the fiancée knows I'm back!

Smiling, smug, ARNOLPHE *knocks three times at this door.* CHRYSALDE *makes the 'he's nuts' sign as he exits.*

CHRYSALDE.
I think my friend de la Touche is somewhat touched…

ARNOLPHE.
He's some Chrysalde! He is too much!
Very opinionated, not a man for listening!
Helluva sure he's in the right 'bout everything.
Haw! HAW!

And ARNOLPHE *knocks again.* ALAIN, *the manservant (he's very very thick), answers very loudly from behind the door.*

ALAIN.
Who's therr?

ARNOLPHE.
Open Sesamee!
This fortnight I've been away she'll fairly have been missing me…

ALAIN.
Who is it?

ARNOLPHE.
Me!

ALAIN.
That you, Georgette?

GEORGETTE *appears on a wee balcony above, but unseen by* ARNOLPHE. *She is by no means as stupid as she initially appears. Above all, she loves winding up* ARNOLPHE – *and her idiot husband,* ALAIN, *too.*

GEORGETTE.

                              Naw!

ALAIN.
You've to open the door, well!

GEORGETTE.

                    Naw, *you*, you big blaw!

ALAIN.
I'm no!

GEORGETTE.
        Well, I'm no!

ALAIN.

                    Neither am I!

ARNOLPHE.

                              Give me strength,
I'm to be standing on my own doorstep for this length!

GEORGETTE.
Who is it?

ARNOLPHE.

        Me!

GEORGETTE.

        Alain!

ALAIN.

                    Whit?

GEORGETTE.

                    It's the Master,
    Hurry up!

ALAIN.
        Naw you!

GEORGETTE.

You dae it, it'll be faster!

ALAIN.

It's your joab, Georgette, I've tellt you before!

ARNOLPHE.

Whichever one of you won't open this door
Will feel the point of my boot up their bloody arse!

GEORGETTE *goes inside to sort it out, rolling her eyes in
exasperation.*

GEORGETTE.

Dae your joab, Alain, c'mon, this is a pure farce,
Your skiving!

ALAIN.

My skiving?

GEORGETTE.

Your skiving, aye!
– *What* are you doing coming now *I'm* doing it, why?

ALAIN.

Why should you do it and get all the thanks from M'sieur?

GEORGETTE.

No, I'll do it.

ALAIN.

I'll do it!

GEORGETTE.

I'll be doing it, that's for sure!

ALAIN.

Bloody won't!

GEORGETTE.

Bloody will!

ALAIN.

Forget it!

ARNOLPHE.

You daft domestics don't bloody seem to get it!
Open up! This is your Third Verbal Warning!

The door is flung open with a flourish by GEORGETTE,
smiling brightly. ARNOLPHE *falls inside. Now the* SER-
VANTS *are outside on the threshold, so furious*
ARNOLPHE *comes back outside too.*

GEORGETTE.

Welcome back, your humble servant, sir, good morning!

ALAIN.

No, *I'm* his humble servant, you're a lazy trollop.
Were it no for respect for the master here I'd gie you such a
        wallop!

ALAIN *takes a swing at* GEORGETTE *anyway, but she
ducks and the blow lands on* ARNOLPHE.

ARNOLPHE.

Ooyah!

ALAIN *flinches*.

ALAIN.

        Sorry, maister!

ARNOLPHE.

                Wheesht, the pair o you!
I'm fed-up to the back teeth, I can take no mair o you.
Calm down. (*Beat*.) Alain, Georgette, how's Agnes?
I mind when I left her… the picture of sadness,
Oh, was she no just? Alain, away and get her,
Till I reassure my darling I didn't forget her.

ALAIN *goes inside*.

How was she without me? Tell me, Georgette,
Was she awful sad and lonely, my innocent wee pet?

GEORGETTE.

Sad? Nut.

ARNOLPHE.
> No!

GEORGETTE.
> Eh, I obviously mean yes!

The wee soul was constantly on the verge of tearfulness.
Miss you? Och, she ver'near took a heart attack
When I minded her how long it'd be till you'd be back.

ALAIN *re-enters from house with* AGNES. *She's heart-
breakingly young, very sweet, very pretty.*

ARNOLPHE.
Och, needlework in hand, ah bless!
Well, I'm back after this long fortnight, eh, Agnes!
Did you miss me?

AGNES.
> Yes I did. Thank God.

ARNOLPHE.
You mean, thank God I'm *back*, pet, sounded odd
The way you put it, but *I* know what you mean to say!
How's about a wee kiss? How are you anyway?

AGNES *dutifully and sweetly kisses him on the cheek, which
he has inadvertently proferred, while shutting his eyes and
puckering up his mouth.*

AGNES.
Fine.

ARNOLPHE.
> Fine, that's nice, what are you sewing?

AGNES *in all innocence holds up her work up to him.*

AGNES.
Lace, on these drawers. Georgette says it's going
To be all the rage and I should get ready my *trousseau.*

ARNOLPHE *is disconcerted of course, embarrassed.*

ARNOLPHE.
     Well, Georgette's no wrong for once, p'raps you should
          do so…

AGNES.
     All right. But lace is awful fancy for my taste.
     No one will ever see them, will they? It's a waste.

ARNOLPHE.
     Good girl!

AGNES.
               I sewed all the buttons on your shirts
     And darned so many socks my finger hurts.

     *She holds up her middle finger in the classic rude sign – still
     in all innocence though. He kisses it.*

ARNOLPHE.
     Your old Uncle de la Touche will kiss it better!
     In you go now, pet, I'll be back later –
     I've got something very important to put to you.
     Yes, Agnes, something very good for you
     Concerning your future and your happiness.
     See you later, sweetness, and God bless.

     *ALAIN, GEORGETTE and AGNES go into their house,
     AGNES with a dutiful sweet curtsey and a smile.
     ARNOLPHE stands alone, quite delighted with everything.
     He smiles at the closed door and moves to his own grand front
     door, patting his pocket for his keys – but before he can go in,
     HORACE, a handsome and upstanding young man, enters,
     does a double take, and runs up to him, hand outstretched.*

HORACE.
     Arnolphe!

ARNOLPHE.
               My God, young Horace!

HORACE.
                         Mr Arnolphe!
     I'm very glad to see you, sir, at last. It is yourself!

ARNOLPHE.
  Well –

  But before ARNOLPHE *can make his 'It's de la Touche now,*
  actually' speech, HORACE *overrides him.*

HORACE.
             My father will be so pleased when I write!

ARNOLPHE.
  How is the Old Bugger?

HORACE.
                              Oh, you know, all right!

ARNOLPHE.
  Glad to hear it! How's the capital? How's big-city life?
  Haven't seen him in yonks, though I see him in the paper.
  You, you were only knee-high to a grasshopper
  When your family moved – and moved up the pecking
       order!
  Wouldn't be me though! Ask me, the city's fecking murder
  If you pardon my French.

HORACE.
                              Oh, c'mon, it's okay…
  But I'm surprised you recognised me anyway.

ARNOLPHE.
  Well, you've grown, and you've grown up, but not changed!

HORACE.
  I'd like to spend time with you –

ARNOLPHE.
                              That can be arranged!
  How long have you been in town, dear boy?

HORACE.
  Nine days

ARNOLPHE.
             Nine days in this backwater, how'd you enjoy
  It so far?

HORACE.

Very well indeed, sir.

ARNOLPHE.

Good!

HORACE.

Dad said: first thing, go see Old Arnolphe, don't be rude.
He's a family friend and he'll help you out of loyalty.

ARNOLPHE.

Help you! He knows you'll be treated like royalty
In my house.

HORACE.

Except I called and you were away.

ARNOLPHE.

Aye, and I'm just this minute back, what can I say!

HORACE.

Dad asked me, would I give you this letter.
But then he sent *me* this one later
Saying he was actually coming here to town,
Something he wanted to 'see to on his own
That would be to *my* advantage', whatever that means, oh
     well,
I was to book him and A.N. Other into the best hotel –
Some chap from overseas who'd made his pile
And Dad wanted to be sure to entertain in style?

ARNOLPHE *has torn open his letter and is perusing it. It's
only idle and automatic, his questioning, nothing loaded,
when –*

ARNOLPHE.

Overseas?

HORACE.

Yes, but from hereabouts originally.

ARNOLPHE.

What's this rich bloke's name?

HORACE.

Doesn't say.

Oh yes… Hen-rique or summat? Ring a bell?

ARNOLPHE.

Never heard of him.

HORACE.

– Oh well,

Apparently both I, Horace, and this town stand to benefit
If I do what Dad says for once and don't make a mess of it.

ARNOLPHE.

Can't think who this can be, he's a dark horse…
Your father I will be *delighted* to see again, of course!
'*I should be more than grateful, sir, if you could help my
   son*'?
It goes without saying! Why so formal? What is he on!
I owe that man so much! Horace, as sure's
You're your father's son, what's mine is yours!

HORACE.

You really mean it? Arnolphe, you're a sport!
To tell the truth I am a coupla hundred short…?

ARNOLPHE *blanches at this, but what can he say? He peels
the notes from his wad and passes them over.*

ARNOLPHE.

Ha ha… think I could refuse you? Never!
To let me help you is to do myself a favour,
Your dad and I are such –

HORACE.

Don't tell him!

ARNOLPHE.

No!

Our little secret! Let's change the subject. So!
Our town's been redeveloped, and since it got its new face,
Tell me, Horace, what d' you think'f the Old Place?

HORACE.

I think all this gentrification's fabulous, don't you?
And the people are so friendly and there's so much to do!

ARNOLPHE.

Say that again! People to do and things to see!
A dashing young blade like you – oh, listen to me
And I'll see you right, son – the local dames are *dolls*
And frankly they're anybody's, if a guy's got the balls
To really go for it, he could go through them like a knife
      through butter.
The married ones first, their husbands are utter
Putty in their hands, man, they run rings around them!
But you'll know this already, how have you found them?
So far? Eh? How many husbands have you cuckolded
By taking those so-desperate housewives to bed?

HORACE.

Well… I've already found it in my heart to dare
To embark, I must confess, upon a love affair.

ARNOLPHE.

Well, this'll be a laugh! I'll get this young fop bragging
And find out exactly whose wife it is he's shagging!

HORACE.

It's very delicate, this is between you and me…

ARNOLPHE.

Course!

HORACE.

            The lady's honour is at stake, you see!
Sometimes talk can spoil things, and once it's out
A sweet secret is no secret – but I'd like to shout,
And shout it from the rooftops, how much I love this girl!
I'm *in love*, it's like in the *songs*, my heart's in a whirl.
No good lest she love me back though – but there, I
      confess,
I flatter myself I've had… no small success!

ARNOLPHE *is laughing and nudging him.*

ARNOLPHE.
Who is she?

HORACE.
Hush, my friend, say no more!
My darling lives over there, behind that door.
She's very sweet and young, she's almost too innocent
Because her old fool of a guardian wants her ignorant
Of the ways of the world, etcetera, as it were.
Total power trip, so he has control over her!
It makes me mad – but maybe you know
This... *de la Zouche*, Scara*mouche*, whatever, so-and-so?
– Or my *Agnes*, ever seen her? –

ARNOLPHE.
Agh! –

HORACE.
This man –
No one has a good word for him – This idiot can –
Would you believe it? – keep my darling prisoner
And cast up to her every little thing he's given her
So she thinks she has to obey him and be grateful.
Oh, he's very *rich*! And he's *old*! It's hateful!

ARNOLPHE.
What a bitter pill!

HORACE.
Arnie, you don't answer!
Surely you know something 'bout this chancer?

ARNOLPHE.
Think I'm... somewhat acquainted with this case...

HORACE.
Describe to me this sleazy bastard's face!

ARNOLPHE.
He's...

HORACE.
An utter idiot, eh?

ARNOLPHE.

Well…

HORACE.
He is, you're saying nothing, but I can tell!
Ridiculously jealous of everything and everyone!
Thinks he can own her, it's not on!
A lovely girl like that! She would entrance you
Too, if you could only see her… any chance you
Could *lend* me any more? Not now but later!
Oh, what you gave already's very useful, sir, but better –
Since the heart of my Agnes is what I'm fighting for –
Plenty dosh in my coffers! Well, in either Love or War
Money is the engine, when a few palms are greased –
What's up, Arnie, you don't look pleased,
Surely you'd not be one to disapprove
Of my plan to first *free*, then *win* my love?

ARNOLPHE.
How could I?

HORACE.
You're just back. I've tired you out!
I'll pop round soon and give you a shout.

HORACE *begins to leave.*

ARNOLPHE.
Am I supposed – ?

HORACE *returns, tapping his nose.*

HORACE.
Obviously, mum's the word
I'd hate to have my precious secret heard.

HORACE *goes again.*

ARNOLPHE.
I'm *shattered*, so I am!

HORACE *returns again.*

HORACE.
>   I mean, by Dad!
This is the most precious secret I have ever had.
Don't let on! He might not be entirely chuffed
If he doesn't think Agnes is good enough.

– And HORACE *finally leaves.* ARNOLPHE *collapses.*

ARNOLPHE.
Was ever an innocent Christian so ill-used?
I'm too good! My generous nature's been abused
And not for the first time – but what a brass neck,
That Horace, to spill the beans like that and not even check
Exactly who it is he's talking to, the twit!
Painful it was, but I should have suffered it,
Encouraged him further and… sorta drawn him out
So that I could know exactly what this is all about
And exactly – ohmigod! – how far it's gone?
Surely nothing *irrevocable*'s been going on?
Calm down. C'mon, away and catch him up,
Laugh, sook in with the young pup
And get that loose tongue wagging – but I fear
I'll find out what I don't want to hear!

– And ARNOLPHE *exits in hot, if hirpling, pursuit of*
HORACE.

Fade to black.

End of Act One.

ACT TWO

Only a little later. An even more agitated ARNOLPHE *comes wheezing back, out of breath.*

ARNOLPHE.
I couldnae catch up with him, but it's mibbe just as well.
I'm in a state, so I am, and mibbe one could tell
Just by the look of me, eh, I'm that agitated?
No, I'm no myself, and I would have hated
To give away what I *mustn't* give away and he doesn't know.
– Because he doesn't! Scheming little so-and-so!
Scheme all he likes, he'll get nowhere fast.
I'm going to get to the bottom of this at last.

ARNOLPHE *knocks the door of the Agnes-house.* ALAIN
opens it promptly, very pleased with himself, GEORGETTE
not far behind him.

ALAIN.
I opened it!

ARNOLPHE.
      Shut it!

ALAIN.
          Shut it?

ARNOLPHE.
               Naw, c'mere
The baith of you useless articles! C' mon, you pair!
Were you in cahoots? Is this how you obey
Your Lord and Master, when he's away?

GEORGETTE.
Ooyah! Don't shout at us! Don't hit him!

ALAIN.
I wonder what Mad Dog has bit him?

During this scene, ARNOLPHE *hits one then the other, then regrets it, tries to cringingly calm them, and himself, so that he'll mibbe find out what he needs to know. He veers wildly and comically back and forth between rage and placatory modes.*

ARNOLPHE.
I just – I'm – I can't – I'm too choked up to speak –
I need to know what went on here last week.
You, you bloody scoundrels, you allowed
A man – don't run away, don't act cowed,
I won't hit you, if you come clean!
Or cast it up either, trust me – I mean
To have the truth, if you just tell me, no rows! –
WHAT THE HELL WAS A MAN DOING IN MY HOUSE?
Eh? Hurry up! Spit it out! Explain! –
Or you will feel the back of my hand again –
Exactly what went on –

GEORGETTE.
                    Ooyah! I'm like that!

ALAIN.
So am I, I'm up to ninety!

ARNOLPHE.
                    – WHAT?
WILL YOU JUST TELL ME! – Oh my God, I'm sweating!
I'm not a well man, I shouldn't be letting
Myself get like this because it's very bad for me.
Take a breath! Breathe deep and regularly...
– That Horace! I can't say how appalled I am.
That prat I've known since he was in his pram! –
Softly, softly! Send up for the girl hersel...
Ask her very nicely, Arnolphe, treat her well
– And she'll tell you everything you *don't* want to know!
Calm down, it's not certain – you two, go!
Fetch down Agnes, tell her – bad idea!
They'll warn her before they bring her here –
Listen, *I'll* go – Alain, Georgette! Wait!

ARNOLPHE *motions to them very strictly (as in 'stay!' to a dog) then goes into the house.*

GEORGETTE.
Poor auld La Touchey's gonnae take an epaletic fit!
Or worse! A heart attack – or stroke!
Whit a hell of a colour he is. Yon's no joke!

ALAIN.
Why keep Agnes out the world and under lock and key
And be that ower-strict wi' her, it seems to me,
As to keep her away from all the other fellas?

GEORGETTE.
Hello! Could it be because he's jealous?

ALAIN.
Jealous? How? What could arouse that feeling?

GEORGETTE.
Jealousy perhaps?

ALAIN.
                              Aye, but why so *beeling*?

GEORGETTE.
Well, jealousy, Alain, is what we call *a passion*
And when one feels it one acts in such a fashion
As to mibbe display *emotion* quite nakedly –
Oh, not on *your* planet, Alain, it's safe to say!

ALAIN.
Getting up to high-do like that! I don't get it.

GEORGETTE.
Well, jealousy makes you jealous and – forget it!
No! I'm gonnae explain. It's very simple:
Say you've got a ... plate of porridge, for example,
It's *yours*, and it's *on a plate*, and it's *hot* –
Going to let some other greedy bastard eat it or not?

ALAIN.
I'm not actually a big porridge hand.

GEORGETTE.

Soup well! Same question! Understand?
Woman is… man's plate of home-made soup
And when one man sees another try and… dip
His dirty spoon – worse, dirty *fingers* – in his bowl
He tends to be no very pleased at all.

ALAIN.

I'm no stupid, Georgette, I hear what you are saying.
Some men, but, when their wives are… playing
Away from home, like, seems to suit them very well
And they are quite taken on with it – and with theirsel?

GEORGETTE.

That's because some men neither notice nor care.
You can relate to that, Alain, I'm shair!

ALAIN *spots* ARNOLPHE *approaching from indoors,*
AGNES *in tow.*

ALAIN.

Here's the maister coming and, don't tell us! he
Looks even seecker!

GEORGETTE.

Pure green. Wi' jealousy.

ARNOLPHE *has achieved an exaggeratedly om-like state of*
calmness.

ARNOLPHE.

A Certain Greek told the Emperor August
That when one is in a state like that one really must –
Lest one do or say anything one would later regret –
Recite, very slowly under one's breath, the Alphabet.
This I have done – and then the nine times table.
Fortunately, concerning Agnes, I have been able –
Despite my understandable anger and proper pique –
To exercise self-control and this self-help technique,
And now, all-smiles, I've brought her down
To take a wee stroll with me about the town.
Come, Agnes.

(*To* ALAIN *and* GEORGETTE.)
> Away in!

They do, sharply.

(*To* AGNES, *taking her arm.*)
> Nice day for a walk?

AGNES.
> Very nice.

ARNOLPHE.
> Lovely!

AGNES.
> Very nice.

ARNOLPHE.
> So talk!
Tell me all your news, pet, how've you been?
– Is that a wee tear in your bonny een?

AGNES.
> The wee cat died.

ARNOLPHE.
> Shame. But it comes to us all.
We're all mortal, and into each life a little rain must fall.
By the by, while I was away, how was the weather?

AGNES.
> Fine!

ARNOLPHE.
> Fine? I thought it poured.

AGNES.
> – Not altogether
Sunny *all* the time, but I thought it was nice.

ARNOLPHE.
> Nice?

AGNES.
> Mm-hm. Though it mibbe did rain once or twice.

ARNOLPHE.
 So were you a wee bit… lonely, sad and blue?

AGNES.
 Me? No, I never feel like that, do you?

ARNOLPHE.
 While I've been away, what have you been doing?

AGNES.
 Knitted you two pairs of socks and did my sewing.

ARNOLPHE.
 The world, My dear Agnes, is a very strange place
 There's talk. There always is. Behind your back or to your
  face.
 Actually, some of the neighbours – and this canny be true! –
 Have been saying that a Young Man has been… paying calls
  on you.
 A Stranger! Male! In my house! And me away!
 As if! *Un*believable! What will they no say? –
 Because I'll lay a wager it's just idle chat.

AGNES.
 Oh Lord, no, you must not bet on that.

ARNOLPHE.
 What? Are you saying a *man* – ?

AGNES.
                    Yes, Uncle dear!
 While you were away he was hardly out of here.

ARNOLPHE.
 Nothing sleekit 'bout our Agnes, hasn't the sense
 To lie about it – which proves her innocence,
 In one way I suppose – (*Coughs*.) I seem to recall
 That I forbade you seeing anyone at all.

AGNES.
 Yes! But though I did see him, the point is: *why*?
 I guarantee in my place you'd have done the same as I.

ARNOLPHE.

Mibbe. Tell me everything, I'm listening to you...

AGNES.

It's incredible! It's amazing! But it's true!
I was out on the balcony – you know, sewing –
When I became aware of someone... to-ing and fro-ing
Below me, back and forth, looking up, and it
Was a young man of the sort Georgette calls fit!
When he saw he'd caught my eye, he smiled
And made an elaborate bow, blushing the while.
I blushed back, and I curtseyed lower still,
He bowed back, then *I*, then *he* – until
(I nearly laughed!) I thought darkness would fall
Before either one of us would give in at all!
We'd be nodding back and forth for ever, if you please,
Rather than relinquish our mutual courtesies.

ARNOLPHE.

Tell me more...

AGNES.

Well, the very next day, Georgette
Came up looking very solemn, goes: 'Agnes pet,
You are a very lovely girl, God made you that way.
But you have to use your beauty *responsibly*
Because you can cause a lot of damage – can't you tell
You have made that poor young man no well?'
I says: 'Me? Why? What have I done?
The last thing I would want to do is injure anyone.'
'Bit late for that,' she says, 'he's smitten.'
I says: 'With what?' She says: 'The boy's forgotten
Who or *Where* or *Why* he is, he's hypnotised.'
I said: 'How did that happen?' She said: 'Your eyes!'
I said: 'I didn't!' She said: 'I told you, your beauty
Pure *slayed* him, laid him low, it is your duty
To provide some remedy or else he'll languish,
Even *die* maybe, such is his anguish.'
I said: 'Oh, what can I *do*?' She said: 'I'm not sure...
Unless seeing you close up might effect a cure?'

I said: 'You really think so?' She says: 'Worth a try.'
– So obviously I had to see the man. That's why! –
I said: 'Georgette, send word to the poor young man:
If he'd like to visit me in my chamber any time, he can.'

ARNOLPHE.

That bitch Georgette, she's a whore-of-Hell, her!
When I get my hands on her, I'll bloody kill her!

AGNES.

See, Uncle, I knew you'd understand
There was nothing disobedient or underhand!
You're like me, you hate to see another suffer
I know you, you'd have been the first to offer.
So he saw me and – instantly – this did the trick.
He blossomed – you'd not know he'd been sick!

ARNOLPHE.

Total innocence again. This is actually quite sweet.
It's *my own absence* that was… somewhat indiscreet
To say the least, leaving the wee soul wide open
To the kind of attacks on her virtue that are bound to happen
With the badyins that are about, and her all alone!
What possessed you, Arnolphe, to leave her on her own?

AGNES.

What's upsetting you, Uncle – don't say you're not!
Did I do something wrong or what?

ARNOLPHE.

No! (at least I hope not)… I'll be quite relaxed
Once I know what the Young Man did next.

AGNES.

Gosh! What *didn't* he…! I was quite blown away
I was ecstatic! Oh, it was… what can I say?

ARNOLPHE.

Just tell me.

AGNES.

          Poor boy! I know he *suffered* –
But recovered beautifully once the cure was proffered.

What can I tell you? The long looks, the wee whispered
   talks,
The lovely present he made me of a trinket box.
And he was that generous with tips to Georgette and Alain.
They said: 'You can tell that young man to come again!'
I promise you, Uncle, you'd have loved him too!

ARNOLPHE.

But when you were alone together, what did he do?

AGNES.

Told me he loved me in no uncertain fashion,
Made me understand this was no ordinary passion
But true love. Forever. I was... over the moon.
I felt dizzy, so I did! A sort of *swoon*
Sort of sensation sort of thing sort of shook me
To my very core and quite overtook me.

ARNOLPHE.

Oh, very good, Arnolphe. It seems to me
You asked for that exquisite form of agony.
(*To* AGNES.) Okay. Sweet-talk and dizzy-turns, any...
   caresses?
Did he bestow on you any (f'rinstance)... kisses?

AGNES.

Oh yes! We were never done! He seemed to love it
And never, ever, seemed to weary of it.

ARNOLPHE.

Kissed you on your lips, and on your face?

AGNES.

Of course. And that was not the only place.

ARNOLPHE.

WHERE DID HE KISS YOU?

AGNES.

                              In my chamber, didn't I
       explain?
Do we really have to go through all that again?

ARNOLPHE.
> Be patient with her. Aaah… Agnes… Sweetness,
> Where exactly… on your person… did he kiss?

AGNES.
> Silly-billy! Going to make me blush but you don't care!

ARNOLPHE.
> Just let's – beat by beat – go through it. Where?

AGNES.
> My hands, my arms, the inside of each wrist.

ARNOLPHE.
> Nothing we can't forgive and live with on that list.
> (*To* AGNES.) Little liberties! Any… emm… *others* that he
> > took?

AGNES.
> Well…

ARNOLPHE.
> > Well, what?

AGNES.
> > > He took…

ARNOLPHE.
> > > > What?

AGNES.
> > > > > Look,
> I just can't tell you because I know you will get mad!

ARNOLPHE.
> I won't!

AGNES.
> > You will!

ARNOLPHE.
> > > I won't, for Godssake! What's he had?

AGNES.
> Swear you won't get angry! Cross your heart and hope to die!

ARNOLPHE.
  I swear, I swear it.

AGNES.
                    No. I can't say it, you'll be furious,
        that's why!

ARNOLPHE.
  Won't.

AGNES.
        Will.

ARNOLPHE.
          Won't! I promise!

AGNES.
                          Really?
  He took... No, he *took* nothing, I gave it freely!

ARNOLPHE.
  What did this young man manage to get from you?

AGNES.
  He... No, I can't.

ARNOLPHE.
                  Just tell me what, and tell me true.

AGNES.
  He took away my little heart-shaped silver locket.

ARNOLPHE.
  Forget the flaming locket! Fuck it!
  Oh, forgive me, Agnes! See, pet, I didn't think it –
  The way you were talking – was a matter of a *trinket*.
  Just: did he do anything but kiss your lips and wrist?

AGNES.
  Why? Are there other places to be kissed?

ARNOLPHE.
  No. No! But – apropos his *malady* –
  He did not suggest any particular remedy?

AGNES.

No. If he should have told me of anything he'd need
In order to get better I'd have, of course, agreed.

ARNOLPHE.

I've got off, it seems, very lightly. This time.
But if I make the same mistake again then I'm
A fool to myself – and I'll deserve all I get.
You didn't mean any harm, Agnes, let's forget
It, mmm? These charmers, though, are *not sincere*
And they'll first love, and then laugh at, you, my dear.

AGNES.

More than twenty times he told me that's not so!

ARNOLPHE.

Yes, but whether he has a conscience you don't know!
Agnes, to accept a trinket box or other minding,
Or listening to all his havers – and, especially, finding
Such wicked joy in that kissing-wrists-and-lips behaviour
Well, *that's* the kind of thing, pet, which Our Saviour
And them-that-brought-you-up would cry a Mortal Sin.

AGNES.

A sin? A *mortal*…? What? How's that again?

ARNOLPHE.

How? A mortal sin's one that's not forgiven
Because it causes such deep offence to Heaven.

AGNES.

Offence? But why should Heaven be offended?
That I could never understand, nay, if my life depended
On it, Uncle dear. It was such a revelation,
This brand new, and oh-so-sweet, *heavenly* sensation.

ARNOLPHE.

Physical pleasure can be sensational, right enough
But you need to be married before you try this stuff.

AGNES.

But it is no sin if you're married, you say?

ARNOLPHE.
It's not.

AGNES.
Then I need to get married right away!

ARNOLPHE.
If that's what you want, that's fine by me.
That's why I hurried back to town, you see!

AGNES.
Really?

ARNOLPHE.
Really.

AGNES.
You'll make me so happy!

ARNOLPHE.
Yes! Matrimony makes one quite the happy chappie!

AGNES.
So the two of us will –

ARNOLPHE.
Yes, definitely!

AGNES.
You'll get such a great big hug and kiss from me!

ARNOLPHE.
Well, yes. And I'll… embrace you back.

AGNES.
Uncle, are you teasing? See, I seem to lack
What they call a Sense of Humour? I never know
When someone's joking. If you are, please tell me so.

ARNOLPHE.
I was never more serious in my life.

AGNES.
Oh! Then – oh happy day! – I'm going to be A Wife.

ARNOLPHE.
  Indeed.

AGNES.
    But *when*?

ARNOLPHE.
          If we go for Special Licence, say next
  week?

AGNES.
  Uncle, I'll be so, so happy. He is… quite unique!

ARNOLPHE.
  Who is?

AGNES.
    He is!

ARNOLPHE.
        He is? Who?
  Who exactly do you think you're getting married to?

AGNES.
  Well, to Him, of course.

ARNOLPHE.
              Yes, that's about to happen. Not.
  You're more than a little presumptuous, I'd have thought?
  I've picked out quite another person as the man for you.

AGNES.
  Who?

ARNOLPHE.
    Never mind! Your Young Man'll find out No Can Do!
  I'm going to keep *you*, in future, on a much shorter leash
  And it's all over between the pair of you. Capeesh?
  Comes sniffin round here again? You'll chuck a stone at
    him! The lot.
  Rain down on him the contents of your chamber pot.
  No more Mr Nice Guy, I'll be in the corner checking
  That you – and those bloody servants – send him packing.

AGNES.
But he's so, so lovely –

ARNOLPHE.
                         Hih! What a speech!

AGNES.
I'll simply never have the heart to –

ARNOLPHE.
                                   Enough, ya wee bitch!
In you go, and up those stairs!

AGNES.
                  But –

ARNOLPHE.
                             But nothing!
I'm the boss and I'm talking, miss, you're listening.

Sobbing, AGNES *goes indoors.* ARNOLPHE *is left there, pointing, the very tableau and image of a raging despot.*

Fade to black.

End of Act Two.

ACT THREE

*Some time has passed and it's now quite late the same after-
noon.* AGNES *is sitting on a garden bench, her head in her
hands, breathing deeply. Chastened,* ALAIN *and* GEORGETTE
*stand, one on each side, looking on with concern. They catch
one another's eye and shake their heads.* GEORGETTE *touches*
AGNES*'s shoulder in sympathy. From indoors enters a calm,
smug* ARNOLPHE. GEORGETTE *scurries back to her place.
Simultaneously,* ALAIN *bows and* GEORGETTE *drops a
curtsey. A clock strikes four and* ARNOLPHE *checks his watch
and smiles.*

ARNOLPHE.
    I'm delighted 'bout how that went. Well done!
    Tickety-boo! You did exactly as directed, everyone.
    Chased off that young seducer goodstyle and, I trust
    Now we won't see him, or his like, for dust.
    Your innocence and virtue, Agnes, were in danger.
    Never again take sweets, or anything else, from any stranger.
    Young men are vile, dear Agnes – believe me, I know –
    And you were on a path of peril with that so-and-so.
    But, nuff said, no real harm done, he's gone –
    Thanks to the force with which you chucked that stone!
    I know, 'cause I was watching, pet, great stuff!
    Still, I think it *is* time we got you married off!
    Stay, we need to talk! And as for you pair –

GEORGETTE.
    Don't hit us! We didny mean it, it's no fair!
    Sir, we'll obey your orders to the letter!

ARNOLPHE.
    From now on you sure will, you'd better!
    If I believed for one moment you were plotters
    With him against me you'd have got your jotters.

But, as neither of you's the sharpest tool in any box
And I know you both got tricked by that young fox,
We'll draw a line under it and say no more.

ALAIN.

You may kill me if ever again he gets through this door!

GEORGETTE.

Never thought they were right for one another,
Sir, I never liked him! Eyes too close thegither.

ARNOLPHE.

Away, prepare supper and make it a good one.
Let's show Chrysalde a well-laid table with fine food on,
Get out the crystal glasses, the silver and the plate –
Tonight we'll have some special news to celebrate.

ALAIN *and* GEORGETTE *bow and go inside*. AGNES
buries herself in her needlework, pretending to sew.

Come, Agnes, put down your needlework and lace.
Turn yourself towards me, c'mon lift up your face –
Can't see into your eyes with your head all bent!
Pay attention! As my auld mither'd say: *tak tent*
Listen: I mean to marry you, Agnes. I do.
I know that you're surprised at this honour, but it's true
And every day, my dear, you'll marvel at your fate.
Yes, you're a poor country girl, my fortune is great,
Yet I mean to make a lady of you – and an honest wife.
I who have avoided marriage all my life!
– Though there was the odd close shave, I must admit.
It'll be strange for us both, but we'll adjust to it,
Matrimony and the comfort of the marriage bed.
Holy Matrimony! Not to be trifled with, tis said!
Agnes, you are young, but a girl of your intelligence
Can learn to be the Ideal Wife, with diligence,
Humility and application to your duty.
Modesty's important too. Don't flaunt your beauty
Which is the husband's – and his alone! – to treasure
As the… jewel in the crown of his marital pleasure.
In short: don't get all dolled up and go out on the town

Because that'd be letting yourself, as well as me, down.
Fidelity is the bedrock of marriage and obviously
You've not just to *be* faithful but be seen so to be.
D'you understand, Agnes? I'm giving my heart
And you in turn have to play your part
In making our alliance a perfect thing.
It's not about the dress, it's not about the ring
(Though you shall have both!), it's about... a mystery
Wherein, conjoined, a man and woman make a single
     entity
One whole, two constituent parts, *together*, not separate –
Though one is the greater, the other subordinate
As God has deemed it. Who should it vex
To accept that there's a stronger and a weaker sex?
Just as the obedient child obeys the father,
Just as the good servant obeys his master,
Just as the willing subject obeys the king,
The lesser bows down to the greater in everything
And the Ideal Wife knows it's right and good
To show her husband all respect and gratitude.
My protection and my trust, Agnes, must be earned
By your *obedience* – clearly there are lessons to be learned
From our recent wee mistakes? Not just yours, mine too!
But it's not just a matter of another talking-to,
I'm no disciplinarian and I don't want to preach.
Nonetheless, Agnes, since it behoves me to teach
You Right from Wrong, not to put too fine a point
On it – well, this wee book won't disappoint!
It's called *Marriage and Married Happiness*
And it's full of sound advice for you, Agnes.
Think of it as you're learning your catechism
With the aim of getting married, not baptism.
Don't just sit there like a stookie, head bowed.
C'mon, sit up straight and read it out loud!

AGNES *looks up at him in horror.* ARNOLPHE *smiles and
indicates she should read the book he's just thrust upon her.
Eventually, like an automaton, in a slow sing-song voice, she
manages –*

AGNES.

'*Marriage and Married Happiness*
Promises to be nothing more or less
Than the best book on the self-help shelf.
The Secret of Happiness lies within yourself.
This book will help you utilise it.
It will teach you about True Love and How to Recognise it.
How to Target Good Catches for Great Matches. What's
    Cool.
How To Get a Rich Husband and How to Keep Him, The
    Rules.'

ARNOLPHE *grabs the book and turns to page one, sticks it
back in her lap, exasperated*.

ARNOLPHE.

Aye, Agnes, that's just the blurb and introduction.
Turn the page and start to read out the ins*truc*tion –

AGNES.

Uncle…

ARNOLPHE.

          Did they not teach you to read?

AGNES.

Yes.

ARNOLPHE.

     Well, these maxims you'll find useful indeed.

Miserably, AGNES *just about manages to continue, peters
out*.

AGNES.

'Rule One: be faithful, one hundred per cent.
Infid… Inf…'

ARNOLPHE *snatches it from her impatiently and reads aloud*.

ARNOLPHE.

             '-fidelity's a no-no! Fool around, sexually
    experiment,
And you'll wonder where your marriage went!

From Kinsey to Cosmo, behaviourologists say, in no
          uncertain terms:
The so-called Open Marriage is a Can of Worms.'
Quite! Once we're married, dearie, I'll explain
A wee bittie 'bout what such things mean…
Stick to your husband! Have no truck
With looking elsewhere – No Young Bucks,
That's Rule One in a nutshell! Now I'd
Like to hear a bit more of this back-to-basics guide?

ARNOLPHE *forces the book back upon her, and makes her
read.*

AGNES.
    'Rule Two… Rule Two, Rule – (*Bursts.*) Oh, Uncle, I'm in
          pain
    I have such a headache –!

ARNOLPHE.
                              Och, a wee migraine?
Well, in you go, pet, lie down a while
And once you wake up you'll have got back your smile!
It's important you are feeling better
Because we've a guest coming to supper later –
Wee bite of something, mibbe a glass of Chardonnay
To introduce my friend Chrysalde to my fiancée?
Oh, take the book! It's full of advice for the heeding
So it'll be perfect bedside reading.

AGNES *flees indoors.* ARNOLPHE *looks around, beaming.*

Agnes. Perfect. Perfect for me, I feel.
Once she's grown up a wee bitty, she'll be ideal.
She's pretty as a picture and good as gold, her.
Plus she's very malleable and I can mould her
Into – I'll say it again – the Absolutely Ideal Wife,
To warm, cherish and make me happy all my life.
That Horace, he *exploited* her, a near disaster –
If I hadn't come back when I did – or he'd worked faster
– Oh, it just doesn't bear thinking about.
But all's well that ends well, it worked out!

And Agnes's only fault was in her innocence
So to be angry with her makes no sense.
But, oh, the overweening vanity of that young blood!
Kissing-and-telling is his default mode
And once again it only goes to prove
How loose the tongues of young men in love.
They are all the same: they sigh, they moan,
Babble as if innoculated with the needle of a gramophone.
They cannot lock a secret in their silent heart – far better
Than the making of love's the boasting 'bout it later!
Consider Bold Young Horace. Yap, yap, yap.
Might have got her if he'd shut his trap!
Makes you laugh to think an… *emotional incontinent*
Is what Women Actually Think They Want!
But here he comes! All bruised and battered.
I'm almost sorry for the soul. He's shattered!

Enter HORACE, *limping and the worse for wear.*

Ah Horace, 'tis yourself! Well, my dear
Young fellow, how goes the love affair?

HORACE.
Well, since I opened up my heart to you, not great.
The proceedings have been unfortunate.

ARNOLPHE.
Dearie me! How so?

HORACE.
                                        Alas and alack,
As luck will have it, the guardian-bastard's back.

ARNOLPHE.
Is that no hellish!

HORACE.
                                – And not just that.
He's somehow got wind of what is what.

ARNOLPHE.
How could he? Must be One Smart Cookie…

HORACE.

Huh! Dunno! But, despite the care we took, he
Knows. Oh, he knows, you know! It's true!
Well, it was my usual visiting hour, so what should I do
But take myself round there, quite the thing.
The servants, normally so friendly, were *threatening* –
That's the only way to describe it. Normally they can't do
    enough
But it was door slammed – bam! – in my face and: '*Get
    Stuffed!*
Get Lost!' – And much, much worse. I mean,
I can't repeat the half of it, twas that obscene.

ARNOLPHE.

The door slammed! Right in your face?

HORACE.

Exactly.

ARNOLPHE.

And *sworn* at? That's a disgrace!

HORACE.

I know. I tried. But all that they would say
Was: 'My Master has forbidden you, so… *Go Away*'
– Or words to that effect –

ARNOLPHE.

Don't tell me you never got in?

HORACE.

I did not. Nor can I see how I will again.
Even Agnes bade me be gone – she looked that sick –
And flung a stone at me the size of a half-brick.

ARNOLPHE.

A half-brick? No!

HORACE.

Mm-hm. With force.
This was for the guardian's benefit, of course!

ARNOLPHE.

Well, I don't see you can assume that's so!
Your love affair's Up Shit Creek, that's all you know.

HORACE.

It's Not Good. Because the bastard's back to thwart me.

ARNOLPHE.

Now, now! *She's* mibbe changed her –

HORACE.

                                    Don't start me!
Man's a monster! Shameless would-be cradle-snatcher.
She wouldn't have chucked it if he didn't watch her,
That's what was going on and I know it for a fact.
The harsh words she shouted out were all an act.
He was in the room and stage-managed the whole thing –
Yes, this de la Touche bugger was *listening*!
But, my lovely Agnes – and this was a surprise
For she's always seemed so guileless in my eyes –
Came up with what can only be called a master stroke.
Harsh words, half-bricks, yes, but here's the joke,
That's not the message she actually conveyed.
Love is quite an education! Because she played
A blinder of a trick I'd definitely have put past her –
Before his very eyes – upon her Lord and Master.
Amazing! Oh, she's quick! What he saw and heard's
Not the whole story. These were her exact words:
'*I know what you want and here's your answer*' – bang –
Half-brick flung hard – to *miss*! – and tied with string
Around it was, would you believe, this letter!
'Here's your answer...' None could better
Her at the double-meaning caper! Such wit
And from a so-called unschooled girl incapable of it!
He wished! You could have knocked me over – well, I fell
Over the step I was so surprised – I'm limping, can't you tell?
Oh, you have to laugh! Agnes plays it perfectly
And the one who has to fuck it up is me!

ARNOLPHE.

Aye, I'm laughing all right...

HORACE.

                              Oh, laugh with us!
This tyrannical bastard, this miserable old cuss,
Can't make her subject to his will!

ARNOLPHE.
  Yes, it's priceless.

HORACE.

                    I know, I'm laughing still!
But, dear friend, I must show you her letter.
Must confide in someone and, who better?
Everything her heart feels, her hand expresses.
She puts it all so beautifully, never dresses
Her feelings up in fancy phrases. It's *meant*.
It's *felt*. It's… so fresh and innocent.

ARNOLPHE (*muttering furiously to himself*).
  You fool. Stupid idiot! What was so great
  About making madam literate?

HORACE (*reading out the letter*).
  '*Dear One,*
  I don't know how to start. I've just begun to realise I've been
  kept in ignorance, so if I write down something wrong,
  forgive me. See, I don't know what you've done to me but,
  since I met you, I know I'll never ever be the same again. I
  can't bear the way I am forced to treat you.'

  – And here she digresses a wee bit to detail
  How he was watching and what her trick entailed.
  I was incensed, I was… but all I can say
  Is the next thing she wrote blew me away!

  '*I love you. Am I wrong to write this? Am I too forward?*
  Am I foolish to say that, when they tell me everything
  every young man says is a lie, I don't believe them? Tell
  me the truth, are you One Who Lies? For if you were to
  deceive me, I truly believe I should die. They say you only
  want one thing and I don't know what they mean, except
  you told me you do want only one thing and that's my
  heart. You have it.'

ARNOLPHE.
  Bitch!

HORACE.
    What did you say?

ARNOLPHE.
          I said A-*titch*
  – Oo – see, I sneezed, excuse me! Nasal itch…

HORACE.
  She loves me! She loves *me*! Imagine, Arnolphe!
  I was going to tell *her* but she said it herself
  And – she doesn't play games! – she said it first!
  I love her. She loves me. I think my heart will burst –

ARNOLPHE.
  Cheeribye!

HORACE.
      Where are you –

ARNOLPHE.
          I'm away!
  Just minded something very urgent must do today!

HORACE.
  You must know *someone* who could give assistance
  With the thorny problem of how to gain admittance?
  See, I'd the servants in my pocket, but now *he's* back
  That's that well and truly scuppered, alas and alack.
  I know you'll help me! Dear Arnolphe, you must!
  You're the only one round here I trust!

  And, ARNOLPHE *being now gone and inside his own front
  door, it slams shut. Shrugging, puzzled,* HORACE *exits.*

  Fade to black.

  End of Act Three.

  Interval.

ACT FOUR

*Some time has passed. It is now a twilight evening with long
shadows.* ARNOLPHE *emerges from the Agnes-house just as
agitated – if more articulate – than when he stormed inside his
own, away from* HORACE.

ARNOLPHE.
    I can't say I'm actually feeling any better
    Than the moment I was forced to listen to that letter.
    I went in – this was hours ago! – tried to read the paper,
    No joy, I was *fuming* about this Horace caper,
    Went over to have it out with her for once and all.
    But, once there, I said nothing at all –
    Just looked at her to see if she was sorry, but no sign.
    Lost it a bit, not clever, but, hey, not by design.
    Home again, to and fro, couldn't settle, how I paced!
    Nothing for it but to go back just now, look her in the face,
    See whether that treachery and cunning *showed*.
    But no. More beautiful than ever! She *glowed*.
    I bottled out again. I couldn't confront her
    Then I told myself I *shouldn't* – don't want her
    To know what I know because it's the only card I've got,
    That the idiot-lover lets me in on the plot.

ARNOLPHE *paces a bit.*

    I choose this girl for reasons totally rational
    And now I've got the turmoil of this passion all
    Boiling up inside me, I'm flabbergasted, so I am, because
    She is *not who I thought she was*.
    Miss Butter-Wouldn't-Melt – for so she seemed to be –
    Has the wit and wickedness to cheat on me!
    The brass neck to write that letter! Oh, it fills me
    With horror to the bottom of my soul, it kills me!
    He's corrupted her! He's been her ruination!

I could go to law, charge him with alienation
Of her affections – and, if there's any justice, I would win.
But the humiliation of publicity would cause me pain.
I love her. To lose her makes me love her more.
It's true. I love her terribly. It's *sore*!
And I wish I didn't, wish I could go off her,
Wish I could punish her and make *her* suffer.
– Yes, and I know the best way would be to let her
Marry the boy-eejit and totally forget her.
Give them six months and, boy, would she resent
His lack of money, lack of sense, and bitterly repent.
But no, I just can't bear to think of him having her,
Hate myself as I do for loving her.
God help me! Love? Look upon the pain of me!
Would you wish this on your worst enemy?

ALAIN *and* GEORGETTE *come from off, laden with gro-*
ceries and wine, and head towards the Agnes-house.

GEORGETTE.
Haw, sir, we've went and done the messages
For your celebration supper.

ALAIN.
                                        They'd a two-for-one on
     sausages!

GEORGETTE.
– Aye, but we got posh stuff out the delicatessen!

ARNOLPHE.
Oh, shut up about the bloody supper, stop messin
Around with totally unimportant stuff!
We have to plan on how to see this Horace off.
Agnes has plans for him and we must stop her.

GEORGETTE.
I think you already learned us good and proper.

ARNOLPHE.
But he can talk you into things, he can deceive –

ALAIN.
That's for sure!

GEORGETTE.
                – But *we're* a match for him, better believe!

Now ARNOLPHE, *acting out the part of* HORACE, *tries it
on with each of the servants alternately.*

ARNOLPHE.
Suppose he goes: 'No *good* man will put up resistance,
My dear Alain, to offering valuable assistance…'

ALAIN.
Your arse!

ARNOLPHE.
         Excellent! 'Now, Georgette,
You're a kindly soul and you'll want to help me, pet – '

GEORGETTE.
Your arse in parsley!

ARNOLPHE.
                Great! 'And now, Alain,
You'll want to be on the side of good, 'cause you're the best
    of men – '

ALAIN.
You're a numpty!

ARNOLPHE.
                Fantastic! 'But we'll die
If you won't help us, so you must, that's why!'

GEORGETTE.
You are a nine-carat, cast-iron tube.

ARNOLPHE.
                        Yes!

Now ARNOLPHE *takes out a couple of coins. When he
bribes each in turn, they take the money and promptly
pocket it.*

'Now, *I'm* not the kind of guy not to bless
Our little transaction with a ... small consideration,
A *pourboire*, as it were, to get yourself a wee libation,
Eh, Alain? And a... wee something for Georgette?
Mibbe get yourself a bottle of fancy perfume, pet?
This is in appreciation of both of your kindness
In granting me access to your pretty mistress.'

Now it gets physical. Each riposte from GEORGETTE *or*
ALAIN *is now accompanied by an ever harder blow after it.*

GEORGETTE.
Ask sumb'dy else!

ARNOLPHE.
                    That's *good*.

ALAIN.
                              FACK OFF!

ARNOLPHE.
Good!

GEORGETTE.
            Aye, gettae Falkirk, ya –

ARNOLPHE.
                              Okay, enough!

ARNOLPHE, *cowering, flinching, puts up 'keys', 'pax'.*
GEORGETTE, *turning on a sixpence, drops the violence. All*
innocence –

GEORGETTE.
Okay, sir, howzatt? Was that spot on?

ALAIN.
Aye, I was wondering how we got on?

GEORGETTE.
– In wurr attempt, sir, to play the good-and-faithful servant?

ARNOLPHE.
You did just fine. Except, I'd... er... want
You to refuse the money. That you must not take!

GEORGETTE.
    No, sir!

ALAIN.
            Never thought of *that*, for goodness' sake…

GEORGETTE.
    Mibbe we should try another dress rehearsal, eh?

ALAIN.
    Well, I'd certainly be up for that anyway!

ARNOLPHE.
    No! That's enough! Now in you two go, okay?

ALAIN.
    You sure? Fancy another shot at it, just say!

ARNOLPHE.
    Go inside! Do what you are told for once!
    Why must you always lead a merry dance
    Around every clear, explicit order that I issue?
    Keep the money! I won't miss you,
    Either – I'll *top* Horace when it comes to tipping
            generously
    When you two *do all you can for me*.

GEORGETTE *and* ALAIN *go in,* GEORGETTE *convulsed
with laughter, but, eyes-behind-her-back style, miraculously
not ever caught laughing when paranoid* ARNOLPHE *whips
around to look at them.* ALAIN, *'reassuring'* ARNOLPHE,
*gives him the thumbs-up, then the V-sign, then a mimed hay-
maker-punch, then the finger, then the thumbs-up sign again
and, grinning 'got it!', goes indoors.*

    Oh, but that Horace is one devious little shit!
    To bribe my servants like that, be not one bit
    Guilty about doing everything he can to steal my bride.
    I'm going to defeat him, though. It's a matter of pride
    Above everything else. He doesn't really love her.
    He just saw her, it was easy, so he had to have her.
    Well, he won't. Never. Over my dead body –

HORACE *enters*.

– Horace, Dear Boy! Is that you, back already…

HORACE.
Oh, Arnolphe, at last! Wait till I tell you,
I had such a lucky escape! Oh, it was Hell, you
Wouldn't believe what I've been through since we last met!
You'd never believe how complicated it could get.
Well, when you left I went by the place they keep her
      prisoner
I thought: I can't wait until I've given her
Somehow, my answer to her letter.
I need to tell her I love her too, I'd better!
So I went by, hoping, and lo! I saw her and a
Wee lapdog playing fetch on the veranda
She let the ball go over, shouted: 'Georgette,
I'm away down to the garden to get it!' 'Okay, pet!'
So down she comes and lets me in the garden gate,
Sends me up the back stairs to her chamber. 'Wait!
Hide in the cupboard till it's safe to let you out.'
I do. But then I hear one helluva shout:
'Agnes where are you?' and in stomps the guardian
Talk about a brute? By God, he's a hard yin!
I couldn't see a thing, of course, stuck there in that press
But I could *hear* him trash the place, some mess!
Kicked over her writing table, smashed her chair,
Threw her pens and paper everywhere.
Agnes is like: 'Uncle de la Touche, what's up?'
But no answer, just kicks the wee pup
For getting under his feet as he storms back and forth.
He grumps and harrumphs, then: 'Ach, you're not worth
Bothering about, you wee besom', and he leaves again.
I was quaking! Agnes opens up the press. 'He's gone.'
I said: 'Yes, but for how long? We can't depend
On him staying gone and how can I defend
You if he should suddenly return?' 'You'd better
Go for now,' says she. I said: 'That letter,
I'm convinced somehow he got wind of it.'

She said: 'Surely not, for I'll not hear the end of it.'
He didn't say so, but, to Agnes's consternation,
As far as I'm concerned it's the only explanation.
Someone's blabbed. The servants, they're who I blame!
Agnes says no, but who *but* them?
Anyway, they know nothing whatsoever
About *this* plan of ours. It's as clever
As it's simple – you'll love this. Tonight
I get a ladder, hoot three times, on goes her light,
She opens her window and up I climb.
In I go, we've – under cover of the dark – all the time
We could wish for, to be properly together
And express how very much we love each other.

ALAIN *comes out of the house with two neat, celebratory*
bay trees in pots, sets them out one each side of door.

Quick! There's the servant! Hide! It suits
Us if he doesn't see we're in cahoots!
God, Arnolphe, it would be a complete disaster
If he clyped about our friendship to his master.
Wish me well, dear friend, I'll better a-
Way and get the ladder, etcetera.

And HORACE *goes off.* GEORGETTE *comes out with party*
ribbons or balloons to join ALAIN. *When* ARNOLPHE
approaches them, they jump in exaggerated alarm.

ARNOLPHE.
My good and faithful friends, help me you must.
I know I have your love, you have my trust,
But it is time we had a demonstration
Of all this *in action* – and on this occasion
I'll definitely make it *worth your while*.
This Horace bugger's got a plan – it makes me smile
To think he thinks he's going to get away with it!
He's going to climb in Agnes's window, the twit!
This midnight-caller, this cocky wee Romeo
Thinks three hoots and a ladder is the way to go!
Owl-signals, *lights*! This would all be great for him

If it wasn't for the fact we'll lie in wait for him,
Each with a bloody big stick or a baseball bat
And we'll give him a good seeing-to with that.
Understand? There'll be a replacement –
Us! – for the one he hopes will open up her casement.
The main thing is: he must not find it
Out – ever – that it's been *me* behind it.

ALAIN.
If it's only a doing you want done
I'll do it goodstyle.

GEORGETTE.
Sir, it'll be fun!
I'm actually quite handy with a stick.

ARNOLPHE.
Mind, keep mum! Away in you go then, quick.

ARNOLPHE *shoos them indoors and begins to childishly
mock and imitate first* AGNES *then* HORACE.

'Only one thing… My heart, you have it.'
'Oh, *wait* till I tell you, Arnolphe, you'll love it…!'
I shall go mad. Obviously, I wanted someone pure
So I went for someone young, just to be sure.
Sure! Only thing that's sure is: *he shan't have her*!
Oh, I hate her. I hate her. I love her.

Enter CHRYSALDE, *carrying a fancy new bottle of expensive whisky by the neck.*

CHRYSALDE.
Will we have a wee malt before we eat?

ARNOLPHE.
No, I'm no hungry, bugger off.

CHRYSALDE.
That's sweet!

ARNOLPHE.
Sorry! Didnae mean to speak my thoughts *out loud*!

CHRYSALDE.
>Am I right to intuit a little cloud
>On your horizon, my dear friend? How's the romance?
>The... May-December Wedding *off*, perchance?

ARNOLPHE.
>That's none of your bloody business, buddy!

CHRYSALDE.
>Tetchy! Oh dear! Crashed and burned already?
>Can see it in your eyes! Has... your Lolita
>Opted for someone younger and sweeter?

ARNOLPHE.
>Unlike certain other people I could name
>I'm not about to just stand by and bear the shame
>Of seeing someone else *waltz off with my woman* –

CHRYSALDE.
>Steady on! To get all worked up is only human,
>I suppose, in matters of the heart... and other organs.
>But why not be philosophical, brother, for once?
>Hurt, devastated, *shamed* – however we feel
>Losing to a rival in love is no big deal,
>Not in the scheme of things. Flood or famine,
>Earthquake, bankruptcy, *death* are worse, so let's examine
>Why, when wounded in love, we *overreact*
>Let's calm down a bit, eh? Let's make a pact.
>We're friends. Let's institute a little give and take.
>You ease up a bit and give yourself a break
>Over this *wearing horns* and *being cuckolded* – you are
>   obsessed!
>Women are human beings, not chattels to be possessed
>Body and mind, thoughts, dreams, desires, heart and soul.
>Some things are – properly – *beyond our control*.
>So lighten up, okay? Can't you see
>*Your* honour isn't tied up in *her* chastity.
>You're hurting. I can relate to *that*, and certainly
>You don't need it made worse by cheap jibes from me.
>So I'll cool it, stop the smart remarks – (as a species
>We're addicted to sarcasm, we're vicious!)

In return: cut out the cracks about my wife's infidelity.
If she strayed – *if!* – then *she came back to me*.

ARNOLPHE.

Oh, that's all right then, no bother!
Just shower off the last traces of The Other
And back you come between the sheets of the marriage bed –

CHRYSALDE.

You're twisting things, that's not what I said!

ARNOLPHE.

You bloodless bastard! I'm completely out the fashion,
Obviously, reacting with a bit of passion!

CHRYSALDE.

Where is it written passion is a virtue?
These feelings, wallowed in, are bound to hurt you –
You and everyone else – they're totally destructive.
I listened to a Man of the World and found instructive
His advice on how to weather such a crisis.
He said: 'Taken-back, forgiven, a wife is twice as
Liable to be forgiving in return.
She's got a lot of Brownie Points to earn.
So she'll – quid pro quo – turn a blind eye on
Any little extra-marital adventures *you* might try on.
And she'll woo you too, if she wants to get you back –
Watch her rediscover her Inner Tiger in the sack!
In private and domestically, she defers to you,
Constantly proving there's no one she prefers to you.
In company, she'll always be modest and polite
And, in the kitchen, always tempting your *other* appetite.'
I'd rather, far rather, live with such a wife
Than be, God help me, stuck for life
With some bag who, because '*she's faithful*', thinks
She can nag, boss you about, lock up the drinks,
Tell you when to come home, and spend all your money.
She'll be ugly as sin, to boot – the kind of honey
No one would try it on with anyway!
Rather my wife than that one any day!

ARNOLPHE.

Thanks for the eloquent harangue.
You're right. I'm obviously wrang.
Everybody would want to be in *your* position, since
Your horn-wearing Cuckold is a Total Prince.

CHRYSALDE.

All I'm saying is: fate is not a matter of your choosing.
One's spouse can be unfaithful without one losing
Every last smidgen of one's self-respect.
Why should it be so fragile? Why connect
The sin of another (which one did not commit)
To one's well-being and suffer so for it?
But shall we eat? Dear friend, I'm ravenous.
What's cooking Chez de la Touche for us?

ARNOLPHE.

Didn't you hear me? Supper's cancelled.

CHRYSALDE.

Only this morning you insisted that I pencilled
In – remember *you* invited *me* – this dinner date!
You said you had something to celebrate.
I told my wife to give my dinner to the dog
Because I was coming round here to go the whole hog –

ARNOLPHE.

Yes, well, Whole Hog's off. Things've changed.
Let's hope another, better date can be arranged.
But tonight there's something I need to nip in the bud
And the last thing on my mind is food.

CHRYSALDE.

Oh!… These things happen, I suppose. Oh well,
Let's hope the kitchen's still open at the hotel.

And, obviously very miffed, pocketing his bottle,
CHRYSALDE *exits.* ARNOLPHE *goes in to his own house.*

Fade to black.

End of Act Four.

ACT FIVE

More time has passed. It is now the middle of the night.
ARNOLPHE *is in total panic outside the Agnes-house.* GEOR-
GETTE *and* ALAIN *are there too, having just reported to him.*

ARNOLPHE.
    Oh my God! What do you mean, 'he's dead'?

ALAIN.
    We just gave him a doing.

GEORGETTE.

                    – Like you said!

ARNOLPHE.
    Don't blame me! I gave the order
    For a mild *sort-him-out* sort of thing, not bloody murder.
    I meant a blow or two across the shoulders,
    Not a crack on the head, a fall *onto boulders*
    From a great height so that he *died*.
    We're all guilty of culpable homicide.
    In you go, you two, and get your story straight.
    It wasn't us! We never heard a thing, don't let
    Them pin anything on us – Oh God, I'd rather
    Do anything than face his father!

    GEORGETTE *and* ALAIN *have already gone indoors.*
    Woozily – warily – HORACE *staggers on.*

HORACE.
    Is that one of the thugs that went for me?

ARNOLPHE.
    – He'll be in bits! (*Beat.*) Who's that? Wish I could see…

HORACE.
    Is that you, Arnolphe?

ARNOLPHE.
                Uh-huh... but *who* –?

HORACE.
    It's me, Horace! I can't believe it's you.
    Now I needn't wait till morning till I ask my favour –
    You're up early!

ARNOLPHE.
                Is it him? Well I never!

HORACE.
    Going for my lover with the ladder was another
    Plan that – initially – landed us in bother,
    Oh, it did not look good for Agnes and me!
    I don't know how they breached the secrecy
    We'd cloaked the whole scheme in, but, hey,
    The vicious bastards were waiting anyway –
    They knew that I was coming, I could tell.
    They set about me. It was brutal. And I fell –
    Fell from that top window to the ground.
    I was winded – what a fright I got – but found
    There were no bones broken, I was right as rain.
    Well, I've a bruise the size of Scotland and a sprain –
    But to say *I was lucky* is to underestimate
    How fortunate I was to dodge the fate
    Which all too easily could have been mine.
    I fell all that way, and – basically – I'm fine!
    Well, what a caterwauling came from above!
    They were distraught! I didn't move.
    Just lay there on the ground, played dead.
    'Oh my God, you've killed him,' somebody said.
    (I nearly laughed – but didn't), held my breath.
    Down came a couple of them, diagnosed death,
    Having felt my pulse and done some nonsense with a mirror
    It was too dark to see right, blaming one another.
    I'm sure one of the bastards was de la Touche.
    He was yelling: 'Who hit him?'; 'Did you push
    Him?'; 'Oh my God, we'll get the jail!'
    And: 'Oh my Christ, they'll hang us all!'

– And, panicking, off they ran into the night.
Then Agnes – she got an awful fright –
Ran out (they'd left the door *open* in the hullabaloo)
Shouting: 'Oh my love, they've killed you. Is it true?'
And clasped my corpse – she thought! – in floods of tears
Until, whispering, kissing, I allayed her fears…
She's not going back! She's run away with me
And tomorrow we will marry, secretly.
Meanwhile, I've got her hidden in my room
– Which isn't far enough away from him,
Not if he puts two and two together
And realises we've run away with one another.
Hence my coming here to ask you for that favour.
I want you to hide her at *your* house, he'd never
Ever suspect that's her hiding place.
Isn't this a brilliant plan? It's ace!
– Plus there's her honour at stake, respectability
That she'd lose if she spent the night with me.
(Although I'd never breach my darling's chastity
Until tomorrow, when we're married properly!)
So – just for tonight – can I bring her over?
At least no one will accuse you of being her lover,
My dear and trusted, venerable friend
Upon whose wisdom and generosity we so depend.

ARNOLPHE.

Thank you. You can indeed depend on me.

HORACE.

I do. Always. But this time I thought: *We'll see…*
– For I feared that you might take my father's part
Since I know how close you hold him in your heart.
I know! My dad… I don't think he'll be pleased.
But later on he'll, won't he, be easily appeased
Once he sees my darling and how fine she is?
How beautiful and sweet and happy to be mine she is?

ARNOLPHE.

I'm sure. Nothing could give me greater pleasure
Than to be entrusted with your lovely treasure.

HORACE.

>An old man on the side of youth!
>Aren't enough like you, and that's the truth!

ARNOLPHE.

>Bring her, quick – it's getting light
>And, be sure, I'll see her right –
>Not, I stress, by the front entrance
>Because she might be seen by servants
>And you know how those domestics *talk*.
>Bring her up that back alley, I'll unlock
>The *back* door and, secretly, we'll let her
>In to where she's just as safe as we can get her.

HORACE.

>You're right. Time's moving on. I better go
>And bring my darling straight to you.

>*HORACE leaves.*

ARNOLPHE (*being left alone*).

>Ah fate! Of late you've been… capricious
>But now – the irony is quite delicious –
>You've turned again to be, quite firmly, on my side!
>Let's don a quick disguise before we greet the virgin bride.

>*But* HORACE *immediately re-enters with* AGNES *in tow, so all* ARNOLPHE *has time to do is pull his cloak up around himself and step into the shadows.*

HORACE.

>– But, Agnes, what were you doing out of my room?

AGNES.

>Your landlord came and I was scared of him!

HORACE.

>Even so, to come out into the dark! Thank God I met you
>And could bring you here. I'll never let you
>Out of my sight again, oh, I'll keep you from harm.
>But you must go – and let this cause you no alarm,
>It's for the best – with this kind gentleman I trust.
>Hush! Just for tonight, my love, you must.

HORACE *puts* AGNES*'s hand into the cloaked*
ARNOLPHE*'s outstretched one, as he reaches from his
hiding place.*

AGNES.
But Horace, please don't leave me!

HORACE.
I won't be long, my darling, believe me.

AGNES.
I'm unutterably miserable without you.

HORACE.
I know, me too.

AGNES.
           I hate it!

HORACE.
                I don't doubt you.

AGNES.
But if you hated it as much as I, you wouldn't go.

HORACE.
Now you know that I do, and you know that isn't so!

AGNES.
Can't possibly love me as much as I do you!

HORACE.
Oh, love of my heart and life, Agnes, *please*! I do too!

AGNES.
Ouch! He's *pulling* me!

HORACE.
              Only to emphasise
The peril we are in, and I don't think you realise!
Our friend has only our interests at heart.
There are Dark Forces, Agnes, who'd tear us apart.

AGNES.
But to go with a stranger who –

HORACE.

– is no stranger!
My trusted friend is saving us from real danger.

AGNES.

But isn't this dangerously close to –

HORACE.

– Your old place?
Well, so much the better. Just don't show your face!
Our friend will hide you and keep you safe.
It'll be daylight soon – I must be off!

And, kissing AGNES *very quickly, he runs off.*

AGNES.

Horace!

ARNOLPHE.

Come on, he'll catch you later!
Come with me, I've somewhere better
To hide you away from prying eyes.
You'll be comfortable and safe here, dear –

ARNOLPHE *drops the cloak from his face.*

– Surprise!

AGNES.

HORACE!!!

ARNOLPHE.

No point in shouting, pet, he's gone!
And left wee Agnes with the Big Bad Wolf here, all alone.
Disappointing, intit? The end of all your hopes.
Because: It's Over. Read my lips.
Still so young, eh? And so full of cute tricks.
As sleekit as anything, giving it big licks
With treachery, and cunning and… plain badness
That I'd never have expected from my wee Agnes.
This is the one who was: '*Uncle dear,*
Where do babies come from? Out the ear?'
Well, it seems you're fairly catching up?

Making *night-time rendezvous* with that young pup.
You're a fast learner! Plenty you've been latching onto!
What school have you been gaun to?
This was the girl who was feart of the dark
And had to sleep with a light on? A sharp remark
Would have her greeting, so no need for a skelp.
This is the girl who chucks back in my face the *Help*
And the *House* and *Home* which I gave her?
A girl like that, who would have her?
Ingratitude. Don't they say, and ain't it the truth,
It's sharper than the serpent's tooth?

AGNES.
Why are you giving me a row?

ARNOLPHE.
                              I'm sorry?
Oh, you're right enough, I'm wrong, don't worry!

AGNES.
I can't see what on earth I've done.

ARNOLPHE.
No? Running off in the night? With a *man*?

AGNES.
– A man who wants to marry me, he says.
I am only doing as you taught me. Please
Correct me if I'm wrong, but I thought you said
You had to marry before you went to bed?

ARNOLPHE.
But I intended to marry you, my dear,
As I think I made abundantly clear.

AGNES.
Yes. But here's the thing. Unfortunate, but true.
As a husband, I prefer him to you.
You described marriage to me at length.
It sounded *horrible*. 'God give me strength!'
Said I to myself, 'I'm not going there!'
Horace made it sound very different, I do declare.

ARNOLPHE.

That's because you love him.

AGNES.

That I do.

ARNOLPHE.

And you have the cheek to tell me so?

AGNES.

Why is telling the truth cheeky or impolite?

ARNOLPHE.

Next you'll be telling me *you have the right*!

AGNES.

I do. At least, rights – or wrongs – are quite irrelevant.
Or so it seems to me! I didn't *want*
To fall in love with Horace. It wasn't something I *chose*.
It was a fait accompli before I took pause.

ARNOLPHE.

But you knew it was your duty to desist –

AGNES.

I can't see how anyone can possibly resist.

ARNOLPHE.

– Even if you know how much it displeases me?

AGNES.

What it has to do with you, I just can't see.

ARNOLPHE.

Nothing! Of course not. It's automatic
That, though you love me not one bit, I'm ecstatic!

AGNES.

I? Love *you*?

ARNOLPHE.

Yes!

AGNES.

Well, no.

ARNOLPHE.

> Why not?

AGNES.

> It'd be hurtful to expand upon it, I'd have thought.

ARNOLPHE.

> Why don't you love me, you ungrateful little bitch?

AGNES.

> Lord, he loses it when I tell the truth, that's rich!
> You're not very loveable, but don't blame me.
> I didn't do anything to stop you being nicer that I can see.

ARNOLPHE.

> I tried. In every way, Agnes, but no joy.

AGNES.

> Maybe that's the point. My darling boy
> Did not have to *try* at all, he just knew –

ARNOLPHE.

> – Knew how to get his evil way with you!
> Wicked little bitch! See how she answers back.
> What a brass neck! Cheek she does not lack.
> Well, perhaps Miss Clever-Dick can explain
> Why – at my considerable expense – I should maintain
> *Her* just so *he* can come waltzing in and steal
> Her from her family that loves her? Get real!

AGNES.

> He'll pay you back. Every last brass penny.

ARNOLPHE.

> Plenty money, has he? Funny, thought he hadn't any...

AGNES.

> Anyway, I'm not sure I've been brought up that well.

ARNOLPHE.

> You'd have been better in the poorhouse, can't you tell?

AGNES.

> I've been working out a lot of stuff.
> On the surface, dear Uncle, you couldn't do enough.

But in fact you went to great trouble and expense
To keep me in, what you could call, Darkest Innocence.
Imagine! An education judged successful in ratio
To what its pupil did not know.
I'm ashamed of my ignorance.
And I'll remedy it when I get the chance.

ARNOLPHE.

You think that daft boy can teach you owt?

AGNES.

I think he can. In fact I have no doubt.
That *daft* boy has taught me love and that's a start.
He can teach my mind as he has taught my heart.

ARNOLPHE.

I'll teach you with the back of my hand.

AGNES.

Do then! That'll really make me understand.

ARNOLPHE.

Aaaagh! I can't. I can't hit her, though I should.
I'm not sure that it'd do any good.
Not in the long run. It's useless.
There simply is no educating Agnes.
She is a woman. The one I thought a child
With a sweet nature, easy to mould.
Easy? Sweet? Malleable? Never.
I was dealing with the female sex. Not clever.
Agnes, I still love you. That's it.
Can you find it in your heart to love me a bit?

AGNES.

If I had it in my heart the one I loved was you
Then loving you'd be simply what I'd do.

ARNOLPHE.

If you just *would* you *could*. Oh, I could shake you!
Please. Forget him, he's gone, it won't take you
Long if you put your mind to it. I guarantee
You'll be a hundred times happier with me.
I see he's… awakened your passions in no small measure,

Nothing wrong with that! It'll be my pleasure
To educate you in the ways of love, initiate
You in the kissing, stroking, licking art – it's great
And – I know what you need – so night and day
I'll be giving and guzzling and nuzzling away
And I flatter myself I can fulfil you.
So make up your mind to love me, will you?
Oh God. Have I to tear myself in two?
Tell me Agnes, what am I to do?

AGNES.

Stop! Uncle, these are *your* feelings. Fine.
But they are – you embarrass me – no business of mine.
I'm sorry – no, I'm *not* sorry – you don't move
Me at all. It's Horace I love.

ARNOLPHE.

Right! That's it. Goodbye. It's over.
I'm finished with you, you'll never
Ever get me to change my mind.
You've had your last chance with me, you'll find.
All I want now is to get you out my sight
And that convent-in-the-country'll be where you sleep tonight.

Enter GEORGETTE, *full of trepidation.*

GEORGETTE.

This cannae be right, Sir... But I'm feart
To tell you: Agnes and the Dead Corpse huv disappeart.

ARNOLPHE.

Here she is! Lock her up now, in your place! Take her!
Won't occur to him to go back there to seek her.
You stay there with her till I get a cab, now watch her!
Let her stew for a while, and mibbe catch her
Breath a wee bit, *think*, and, let's hope, catch on
To what's what with this *love* carry-on.

GEORGETTE *takes* AGNES *back to the Agnes-house. As
soon as they are gone in,* HORACE *enters in a terrible state
and bumps into* ARNOLPHE. *Very slowly over all the next
scene, it comes up to dawn and then gradually daylight.*

HORACE.

>Fate's turned against me! Arnolphe, my friend,
Sorry to bother you, but I'm at my wit's end.
Whatever the hell I've done to offend Heaven above
Somebody up there wants to tear me from the one I love.
My father – mind that letter? – has just arrived in town
And with that bigshot from abroad, not on his own.
– Rich bastard! All tan and teeth, looks a real hood! –
Remember, the one who was supposed to do *me* good?
Huh! To my *advantage*? A *life sentence*, total miscarriage
Of justice at that. Yes! *An arranged marriage*!
Me? I'm just the bartered groom and have no say!
Dad says: 'It's going to happen anyway.'
This guy – Henrique's his name – 'member, meant nothing
>　　　to you? –
Well, it's his only daughter they want to marry me to –
And '*toot sweet*'! I nearly died. I was appalled.
Henrique's like: 'Want to know what's she's called?'
I go: 'No!' He goes: 'Not want to meet her?
Sit down, son, have a drink, then we'll all go and greet her.'
Dad's like: 'Get used to it, Horace, I'm sure she's charming.'
I was – literally – struck dumb. A more alarming
Prospect I simply could not envisage.
To lose my Agnes and take another's hand in marriage!
I fled. I did. I thought: go to Arnolphe, he's on your side!
Get him to tell your father you've already met your bride,
Agnes is the only one for you and that is that.

ARNOLPHE.

>Okay, calm down!

HORACE.

>　　　　　　　You can persuade him to – what? –
At least postpone it for a bit? He'll listen to you!
And I'll get a chance to work out what I'm going to do.

ARNOLPHE.

>No bother.

HORACE.

>　　　　Arnolphe, you're my only hope!

ARNOLPHE.

    I'm your man!

HORACE.

                I know and, believe me, I look up
    To you a million times more than I do my real father.
    But, Christ, Here He Comes – together
    With some other cove – yon's not Henrique!
    Get him, please, to put it off for – say – a week…?
    Aargh! We've not had the chance to work out our
        stratagem –

ARNOLPHE.

    Quick! Hide! Trust me to take care of them!

    *ARNOLPHE drags HORACE to a place where they can
    remain hidden (though not from the audience). Once they
    both are, enter CHRYSALDE with ORANTE, an urbane
    gentleman, HORACE's father.*

CHRYSALDE.

    Orante, I can't believe it! You and the long-lost Henrique!

ORANTE.

    I know. He said to me: 'First thing I'll seek –
    After we're fed and rested – is news of my brother
    And, God willing, we'll be reconciled with one another.
    A silly quarrel,' he said: 'twenty years ago! I was a hothead
    Very arrogant in those days, there was a lot said.
    I for one, my dear Orante, most heartily regret
    And I wish Chrysalde could forgive,' he said, 'if not forget.'

CHRYSALDE.

    Can't remember what we quarrelled over. I had a stubborn
        streak
    And, to my shame, cut off all contact with Henrique.

ORANTE.

    Sounds like you and Henrique both rue the day
    You allowed this bitterness to split your family.
    Henrique and I were new-arrived in that hotel.
    'I'd give anything,' he said, (tears began to well

Up in his eyes!) – '*anything* to see Chrysalde' – and *who*
Should walk in to that dining room, but you!
Oh, I shed a tear too, to see you fall upon each other,
Unravel old misunderstandings, brother to brother,
Be truly penitent and at last make peace.
So: Orante here's Only Son and your New-found Niece,
What do you think of this marriage plan?
Tell me honestly, man to man.

CHRYSALDE.

Orante, I can't see how you could begin to feel
That this union is other than ideal.

ARNOLPHE.

Okey-dokey, son, I'll sort it, leave it to us.

HORACE.

But careful that he –

ARNOLPHE.

             Don't make a fuss!

Hey Orante!

ORANTE.

           Arnolphe! How nice to see you!

ARNOLPHE.

I'd've known you anywhere, could only be you.

ORANTE.

I'm here to –

ARNOLPHE.

           I know exactly why.

ORANTE.

How?

ARNOLPHE.

        Yes, I know what brings you here, oh aye!
But: (*Beat.*) Your son is totally against this match,
His heart is otherwise engaged, and that's the catch.
He asked me to vigorously dissuade you

But… (*Long beat.*) No, it is my duty to persuade you
To *insist*. The young are too much indulged, it seems to me
And you ought to exercise Parental Authority
Over this young pup. Orante, go the whole hog
And *make* him marry, even if she's a dog.

HORACE (*still from his hiding place*).
Traitor!

CHRYSALDE.
Come now! Orante, this stinks –

ARNOLPHE.
Oh, we all know what Mr Laissez-Faire thinks
Before he opens his mouth! '*Oh, we should never
Force them if they don't want to. Whatever!*'
And he's right! The father *should* be governed by the son.
This is a truism obvious to everyone.

CHRYSALDE.
– I should say: *stinks of self-interest…*

ORANTE.
Perhaps, Chrysalde, our friend knows best?

ARNOLPHE.
I do. You have made a promise, and your son oughter
Just fucking marry the millionaire's ugly daughter.

Noises off. An almighty crash and the breaking of glass.

ORANTE.
You are so right about my honour and my word.
If I can't make him, I'll look absurd.
And that's about to happen! They will wed.
Can't control my own son? Never let it be said!
– Not that she's ugly, necessarily. Why should she be?
– Though we've yet to clap eyes on her. We'll see!
And, yes, Arnolphe, she is the Daughter of a Millionaire…

CHRYSALDE.
Orante! *Don't* call him Arnolphe or he'll go spare!
It's Mr de la Touche, I told you already.

ARNOLPHE.
 Ach, forget it –

Appalled, HORACE *steps out of his hiding place.*

HORACE.
                    WHAT??

ARNOLPHE.
                         Hold it, son, steady!
 So the Big Secret's out. Take it on the chin
 And think twice afore you blab like that again.

HORACE.
 You absolute –

HORACE *takes a swing at* ARNOLPHE, *but is restrained
by* CHRYSALDE.

ORANTE.
                    Horace! What are you doing here?
 I've been looking for you everywhere!

HORACE.
 To *introduce me* to your bloody heiress?

ARNOLPHE.
 Tut-tut! *Honour thy father...*? He could care less!

Enter GEORGETTE *at great speed, in a panic.*

GEORGETTE.
 Haw, sir, Agnes has totally lost the plot!
 Sir, gonnae come and help us or not?
 She's gonnae do herself an injury. See, I doubt,
 Now she's broke the blinkin' windae, she's gonnae jump out!

ARNOLPHE.
 Bring her here. I'm going to take her away.

GEORGETTE *goes back into the Agnes-house.*

 Ach, don't worry, Horace, son, don't they say
 A reversal like this is *good for you*? Have you forgotten,
 Continuous good luck would spoil a man rotten?

HORACE.

> God in heaven! What a hellish thing.
> This simply cannot be happening...

ARNOLPHE.

> One wedding I'll dance at! Hasten the day!
> Any... wee minding you'd like? Just say!

ORANTE.

> Oh, they *are* going to marry. You're invited!

Enter GEORGETTE *with a defiant* AGNES, *her wrists restrained.*

ARNOLPHE.

Ach, c'mere,

> My headstrong beauty, my stubborn wee dear.
> Here's your ex-boyfriend, wave him ta-ta.
> Cheerio Horace! Never worked out, did it, ha-ha!
> Where do you young lovers get off depending
> On all romances to have a happy ending?

AGNES.

> Horace, are you going to let him take me away?

HORACE.

> I'll die before I lose you!

ARNOLPHE.

You don't say!

AGNES.

> I'm going nowhere.

ARNOLPHE.

Oh, is that right?

> I think, if I say so, you just might.
> Willnae marry me? You'll no marry anyone.
> You'll live in the country – and you'll live like a nun.

ORANTE.

> Mr Arnolphe de la Touche, I think I'm owed an explanation!
> Your... connection with this child causes me some
>   consternation.

From now on, ARNOLPHE*'s real suffering begins. It builds,*
revelation upon revelation, and he has not one word to say.

CHRYSALDE.

Orante, once Henrique made clear to you and me
Arnolphe's impoverished young ward Agnes's real identity
I knew I should let you see for yourself, not mention
What I already knew of Arnolphe's intentions.

ORANTE.

– Somewhat *unsavoury* intentions! Fine kettle
Of fish! Old man, young girl? One's shocked a little…

HORACE.

Not just treacherous, how *lecherous* you've been!

AGNES.

My *real identity*? What can he mean…?

CHRYSALDE.

Must be a bit galling, Arnie. You were urging
Orante to marry Horace to this very virgin!
But let me fill you in. Henrique, my brother
And I were brought up apart. Our mother
(We had different fathers) married twice.
After *my* father died she remarried and suffice
It to say my stepfather – a country laird – wasn't too keen on me
So Mum had me brought up by *her* family –
Her parents, in fact – as if *they* were my mum and dad
In town here. Better a boy could not have had –

ORANTE, *from now on, is constantly trying to hurry on the*
garulous and overexpansive CHRYSALDE.

ORANTE.

– But *anyway* –

CHRYSALDE.

                    My mother and Henrique Senior
Eventually had another son, five years my Junior –

ORANTE.

– Henrique!

AGNES.

> …Horace…?

HORACE.

> Agnes, dare we hope –

ORANTE.

> – Yes, hope!

Chrysalde, perhaps you can hurry this story up?

CHRYSALDE.

> Sorry! Henrique Senior died. Widowed, my mother
> Sent for me to finish my education with my brother.
> Fine! Till, as young adults, we had that stupid row
> And haven't seen hide nor hair of one another till now.

ORANTE.

> In short: Family loses everything and young Henrique
> Goes abroad and never returns until last week.

CHRYSALDE.

> – Complete with fortune! Riches beyond avarice!
> Horace, Agnes, can you get your heads around this?
> Eighteen years ago, and unbeknownst to me, a babe-in-arms –

CHRYSALDE bows before AGNES, smiling, indicating the identity of that babe. Full-blown delight and hope begin to blossom…

ORANTE.

> – Young Henrique, having fallen for the charms
> Of a certain local beauty, so he tells me, in that land
> Who bore him a daughter, got sick and in the end
> Died –

CHRYSALDE.

> – Breaking Henrique's heart. He couldn't cope
> So sent this mite back to our mother in the hope
> That, back home, she could bring up well
> This daughter he loved more than tongue can tell.
> Mum told me nothing, she knew better
> Than mention Henrique to me! And later,

Once *she* died – and this was long before
Henrique hit pay dirt, so she died poor –
The child, *sans* identity, ends up in a country orphanage
Which, as it happened, was under the patronage
Of Arnolphe, who, out of the goodness of his heart,
Being childless –

ORANTE.

              – thought he could provide a start
In life for our lovely Agnes here!
Oh, looks like he's done splendidly, my dear.

CHRYSALDE.

Henrique, not knowing your whereabouts, was devastated
And, once he had the money, instigated
An international search by a top detective agency
Who followed the trail –

ORANTE.

           – and: Here She Be.

AGNES *and* HORACE *fly into each other's arms and kiss.*
ORANTE *and* CHRYSALDE *look on, laughing fondly,*
shaking their heads, delighted.

CHRYSALDE.

– But the truly marvellous thing we did not realise
Was that my niece Agnes was the very one your Horace's
     eyes
Had lit upon in love, Orante!

ORANTE.

           I know! It's odd.
Almost makes one believe in a beneficent God
Ordering all things, in the best of all worlds, for the best.
Well, anyway, that's it all sorted out at last!
No thanks to Horace…! But, hey, all's well that ends well!
So now, Agnes my dear, let's haste to that hotel
Where, bathed, rested and restored, your father waits to greet
     you
– You and Your Intended. Be over the moon to meet you!

Exit, led by a fulsome ORANTE, *without a backward glance at* ARNOLPHE, AGNES *and* HORACE, *the young lovers, entwined.* CHRYSALDE, *though slightly out of their family group, seems to be going with them all too, but, just as he's about to exit, can't resist coming back to have his final say to the shattered* ARNOLPHE.

CHRYSALDE.
Dearie dear, to have your hopes so dashed by this cruel blow.
You feed, clothe, educate and groom this girl, just so
That young fellow can waltz off with her! Best-laid schemes,
Eh? You were going to get a girl like that? In your dreams!
Oh, I know, I know, rejection hurts. And yet,
Since being-cheated-on's your nightmare fate,
(And, the world being how it is, it is aye a worry!)
Well, the one sure way of avoiding it is Not To Marry.
Arnolphe, you can't have everything in this life.
Think I'll away home for a wee dram with the wife!

And, whistling, off goes CHRYSALDE *in the other direction from the wedding party.* GEORGETTE, *still watching from her corner, is the only one left now apart from* ARNOLPHE. *She speaks as if he, the so-called master, isn't even there.*

GEORGETTE.
Wanted to marry wee Agnes? How *could* he have thought her
Likely to make him happy? Young enough to be his daughter!
Ach, there's no fool like an auld fool! – Haw, Alain!

ALAIN *appears on the balcony with a daft, impatient look.*

ALAIN.
Whit?

GEORGETTE.
What is that Arnolphe like, eh? (*Beat.*) Men!

GEORGETTE *goes into the house. Simultaneously,* ALAIN *shrugs and goes in from the balcony.* ARNOLPHE *is left, all alone, suffering.*

Fade to black.

The End.

A Nick Hern Book

Educating Agnes first published in Great Britain as a paperback
original in 2008 by Nick Hern Books Limited, 14 Larden Road,
London W3 7ST, in association with Theatre Babel

Educating Agnes copyright © 2008 Liz Lochhead

Liz Lochhead has asserted her right to be identified as the author of
this work

Cover image: Sarah Lawrie, photographed by Douglas McBride
Cover design: Ned Hoste, 2H

Typeset by Nick Hern Books, London
Printed in the UK by CPI Bookmarque, Croydon CR0 4TD

A CIP catalogue record for this book is available from the British
Library

ISBN 978 1 85459 533 1

Mixed Sources
Product group from well-managed
forests and recycled wood or fiber
www.fsc.org Cert no. TT-COC-002227
© 1996 Forest Stewardship Council
FSC